THE LOST DIALOGUES

BEING A FAITHFUL ACCOUNT OF THE ABSENCE OF
SOCRATES FROM ATHENS BEFORE HIS TRIAL.

Cover design and illustration by Matt Touchard
Destrehan, Louisiana

THE LOST DIALOGUES

BEING A FAITHFUL ACCOUNT OF THE ABSENCE OF
SOCRATES FROM ATHENS BEFORE HIS TRIAL.

Charles Walters

Acres U.S.A.
Kansas City, Missouri

THE LOST DIALOGUES

Copyright © 1994 by Charles Walters

Acres U.S.A., Publishers
Box 9547, Kansas City, Missouri 64133-9547

ISBN: 0-911311-42-4
Library of Congress Card Catalog: 93-079265

Dedidated to all who seek virtue.

Wherefore, O judges, be of good cheer about death, and know of a certainty, that no evil can happen to a good man, either in life or after death. He and his are not neglected by the gods; nor has my own approaching end happened by mere chance. But I see clearly that the time had arrived when it was better for me to die and be released from trouble; wherefore the oracle gave no sign. For which reason, also, I am not angry with my condemners, or with my accusers; they have done me no harm, although they did not mean to do me any good; and for this I may gently blame them.

Still I have a favor to ask of them. When my sons are grown up, I would ask you, O my friends, to punish them; and I would have you trouble them, as I have troubled you, if they seem to care about riches, or anything, more than about virtue; of if they pretend to be something when they are really nothing—then reprove them, as I have reproved you, for not caring about that for which they ought to care, and thinking that they are something when they are really nothing. And if you do this, both I and my wsons will have received justice at your hands.

The hour of departure has arrived, and we go our ways—I to die, and you to live. Which is better God only knows.

—*Socrates' final words at his trial.*

TABLE OF CONTENTS

A NOTE FROM THE PUBLISHER

It has always been the role of the novelist to make the final statement for any historical era. Not one scholarly tome has recorded the agony and pathos of the 1930s half as well as did John Steinbeck's *The Grapes of Wrath*. Arthur Koestler's *Darkness at Noon* gave the world its first real insight into the workings of the Soviet political state, and George Orwell made clear for all with the wit to see how Neanderthal perversion rules the bureaucratic mind. I have always figured that novels merely benchmark the human record, always being too tardy to confer rational behavior on the whole. It never occurred to me that a novelist could handle economic affairs, at least not before the appearance of Leonard Lewin's novel, *Report From Iron Mountain on the Possibility and Desirability of Peace*. Leonard Lewin's topic was the same one I covered in the non-fiction work, *Unforgiven*. It was based on a study commissioned by Robert McNamara during the last year of the Kennedy administration. By then the Kennedy brothers had concluded that agriculture must be despoiled no further. The Vietnam exercise in profit creation for the military industrial complex had to be terminated. The business of substituting parity war for parity agriculture had to be brought to a close—but how? *Iron Mountain* reported back that fully 10% of the output of the world's economies was dedicated to war. The cold war, cleverly choreographed to benefit the merchants of death, cost $6 trillion, approximately the amount of the national debt if honestly reported. *Report From Iron Mountain* was a novel just as *The Lost Dialogues* is a novel. And good fiction contains its own truth. No one from the pantheon of historical figures could be counted on to tell the truth—to bless discourse with the virtue of knowledge—more than Socrates of ancient Greece.

He was a gadfly to the powers that be, a Gandhi-like figure who never held office or sought to lead if only to avoid the wretched compromise of office. Through a long and distinguished lifetime, he exhibited both independence and coldness of judgment and formed up his answers without reference to a higher approved authority. His holy grail was virtue, and his open sesame to life was philosophy. Not without reason, Christianity confered on Socrates the status of pre-Christian martyr. Dante placed him first in the philosophical family. And the sheer power of his reasoning has confered on him the status of civilization's analyst. Still, Socrates was no egghead, even though Xantippi's nagging made him appear as such. He came aboard the stream of things when Athens was powerful at the time of the Peridean period. He was born in B.C. 469, the son of a sculptor and a midwife. Historian's tell us that he was possessed of fantastic physical and moral courage. He served in battle with great distinction and faced down mobs alone, like some ancient Wyatt Earp. He educated himself and endured the evil of lessers. Nowadays—if he had money—he might be considered an eccentric. He wore the same garments winter and summer, and walked without sandals in the marketplace. He spent most of his hours teaching and meditating. Men of intellect found him sensitive and kind; others became bored with him, as mediocrity is want to do. Alone among mortals, Socrates seemed capable of reading humanity's cosmic march. The gadgets of industrialization could not tempt him, for virtue is virtue. Much like the measurement of intelligence, virtue survives sophistry and the mundane, as *The Lost Dialogues* readily attest. The Foreword to this novel sets the stage. The scrolls containing the several dialogues do the rest.

FOREWORD

The *Lost Dialogues* were discovered on July 1, 1930, precisely at the time C. Leonard Woolley captured the world's attention with his excavation of the royal cemetery at Ur of the Chaldees. Woolley's digs were real, replete with so many artifacts a special train had to be tracked to the excavation site, both to serve two hundred workers, and to haul away ancient loot. For this reason and for several other reasons, including a world depression, scant attention was paid when a Greek employee at the Acropolis found a sealed, albeit cracked jar containing no less than *ten* small scrolls and fragments.

No one has ever pretended to know how Socrates of Athens became identified with this discovery. For many years it was believed that "another" Socrates, not the philosopher of B.C. 500 and thereabouts, was the man named in the strange document. In any case, the text made little sense to the busy archivists who deciphered the first few passages. So they put the whole jar of scrolls aside.

It was not until carbon dating was developed in the late 1940s that *The Lost Dialogues* were "remembered" and authenticated as to age. Carbon dating is based on the proposition that anything that once lived—plant, animal, or human being—has a radiocarbon content, the ratio of which is disturbed at death, and decays at a precisely determined rate. The earliest computations for radiocarbon decay, developed by the discoverer of the phenomenon, Williard F. Libby, was arrived at by trapping the gas released by combustion of the sample, then calibrating the Carbon-14 content as compared to the more stable Carbon-12. A special Geiger counter provided an assist. Even this crude method ratified the suggestion that *The Lost Dialogues* dated back to near B.C. 500, give or take 100 years. Later, scientists learned how to convert the tested material to a pure carbon pellet. This pellet of graphite, with cesium, argon and some two million volts of electricity, made it possible to actually count the Carbon-14 atoms. When results were returned from a Los Alamos laboratory to the National Archives in Athens, they confirmed the earlier gas readouts and refined the standard deviation. The scrolls, inked on a special paper made of ditch weed, *Cannabis satavia,* and flax, *Linum usitatiasium,* were indeed as old as Socrates.

This proved to be a puzzlement, for the contents projected at least ten or twenty years beyond the calendar date of the most recent Carbon-14 exercise. No one, not Albert Einstein, not Robert Oppenheimer, not even H. G. Wells—certainly not Roy Kerr and E. Newman of Kerr-Newman black hole fame—could suggest how the philosopher Socrates might have broken the bonds of time. Isaac Newton considered time absolute. After all, matter creates gravity, therefore matter controls space and time, with or without black holes.

It was postulated in the early 1990s that via time warp or black hole or wormhole, Socrates somehow journeyed to the United States, returning with dialogues on sulfite paper that scribes remanded to quality rag-linen scrolls of ancient origin, probably at the direction of the wily Socrates himself, 1990s paper being that substandard.

The black hole idea came from Karl Schwarzs[*black*]child, a German astronomer who described it in 1916 based on Einstein's postulates. In theory the Schwartzschild hole warps space into a wormhole, creating a subway of sorts to other points and other times.

The laughter this suggestion elicited in the news magazines can be hardly imagined. And yet there remained the scrolls and their devilish contents. How they were transported to ancient Greece with a scenario that even now makes them sound futuristic may never be known. Still they are documents for our time. Perhaps we must set aside the complaint by Edward Farhi of Massachusetts Institute of Technology that any escape from time's bonds suggests paradoxes that have no place in physics. "You could go back [in time] and kill your parents before you were born," he said. "Obviously that can't happen."

But ideas are not fenced in by time. Thus we accept as real the dialogues that make up the body of this text. We are prone to look down on the ancients for their lack of improvement in the state of the arts. Perhaps Socrates gave us a clue we too often ignore when he reminded us that the ancients knew the circumference of the Earth long before it was rediscovered several centuries later. Perhaps they knew even more.

These exchanges speak for themselves. That they baffle us as much with their content as does their origin is merely mute testimony, as Socrates would have it, to our lack of *virtue*.

1.

We cannot know the full extent of the dialogue that passed between an unidentified "oeconomist" and Socrates on the occasion of the meeting reported herein. Several wraps of the scrolls "document" had passed through the intestines of an unknown bookworm species that favored the special paper used for important records in Socrates' time.

The first discernable words in the scrolls, "And now, O Socrates," appeared as "in a glass darkly," and then the script grows stronger in full daylight.

AND NOW, O SOCRATES

OECONOMIST. And now, O Socrates, are you ready to say, "Only in America!"

SOCRATES. Of course, I know all too little of your cities and states! Oh, I have passed through your libraries, and I am flattered to find my memory enshrined therein. I have walked this Earth these seventy years, and I can tell you that knowledge cannot be deduced from the past alone. Look at your own universities. Can you not see that all your doctors of philosophy are proof that their science has no understanding of the soul whatsoever? Your nation's health profile will tell all who wish to see that the academies of medicine know nothing about health care and even less about sickness. I can rest my case without argument when I announce that oeconomists know nothing about wealth, or even distribution. And the theology mankind has fastened on the race has canceled out any real knowledge of the gods, or even your universal God. There is only one discipline that has proved itself, for which reason it has been proscribed from your republics of learning, namely logic. If by some great misfortune I should have matriculated from *the university*, generically speaking, then I should be helpless—unless I knew logic. I, like your own oeconomists, would be lost in endless calculations, and could never avail you of an answer. But since I am totally ignorant of your arcane writings—your *Economic Indicators*, your *President's Economic Report*, yet schooled in deathless logic and mathematics, I am able to supply answers at once. Only explain what you perceive, and I will respond. You may think this odd. I assure you that it will be odder still that I am correct. No, I cannot genuflect to your statement, "Only in America."

ƆECONOMIST. Then ask your questions, O Socrates, and I will answer as best I can. Perhaps you can dissect each answer with the stone cut of your logic. Perhaps we can both learn via the exchange. I respect that you know nothing of our economics, the concept being unknown in your ancient Athens.

SOCRATES. This is not entirely true. Your term, *economy*, came into the English language from two Greek words, *oikos*, meaning the house, and *nomine*, meaning to deal out. Originally the term meant the art of managing a farm household. As the farm household became able to support cities, political economy came into being. The chief goal of the city was to take the food production from the yeoman, giving him very little in return. I recall a young man who came to me for instruction in statecraft. He had the build of a god, was blonde as the snows on Olympus, as muscular as a discus thrower. But, alas, he was as dense as an artist's granite between the ears. I asked him how much wheat was required to feed Athens for a year. The young man stood silent. The interview was over. No one can aspire to statesmanship who is totally ignorant of the problems of wheat. So pardon me, I do know something about the oeconomist's craft. I merely restate the proposition that previous experience holds no key to understanding unless logic is invoked.

OECONOMIST. Very well. Then "only in America" has little meaning in terms of what you see? You do not think our course correct?

SOCRATES. I will require you to answer your own question. For now it will be enough to recall that we Athenians were the first to discover the correlation between land and wealth, whereas you have adopted a most illogical metaphysical origin to wealth. Food for people and for commerce with other city-states originates on the land, the source of wealth. Even gold comes from the land, and therefore the true unit of measurement is the land and its raw products. To understand me, you must know how I think.

OECONOMIST. But we have read your ideas and we know how you think.

SOCRATES. Yes, yes! I have seen your great storehouses for books, and I am flattered, indeed, to find my thoughts and words recorded accurately, more or less, by Aristotle, Plato and Olympiodorus. I am also chagrined to learn via Plato, Crito and *Phaedro* that upon my return I will be brought to trial and required to end my mortal existence by drinking a cup of hemlock. So be it. Oh, you think you know me because of these scribes and philosophers. Xenophon's *Memorabilia* makes coins for your purveyors of literature, and, I, Socrates, am handed over to your critics as banal and platitudinous. Aristophanes treated me fairly in *The Clouds*, and I even rate most honorable mention in those matchless comedies, *The Birds, The Frogs* and *The* Wasps. So take your choice. Do you now speak to an Xenophontic, a Platonic, an Aristophanic or an Aristotelian Socrates?

OECONOMIST. Which, indeed?

SOCRATES. You will have to invoke logic and restrict your discourse to the subject you think I know least about. It is by doing thus, and only thus, that you will discern not only the real Socrates, but also the answer to your most pressing paradox. Answer my questions, and I will answer yours. Using the art of dialogue we will reason together, and we will discover virtue.

OECONOMIST. Very well.

SOCRATES. For instance I read in your local tocsin that there will be a tax burden to all citizens of the realm so that free trade can proceed. How do you define this thing, free trade, which is thus promised and for which so great a burden has been contracted?

OECONOMIST. Under free trade, the several countries of the world will be able to sell freely in the United States. By accepting foreign goods, we, in turn, will be permitted to sell everywhere in the world.

SOCRATES. Then your merchants prefer to sell to foreign countries because to sell locally is ill-omened?

OECONOMIST. Not exactly, O Socrates. Some nations produce certain products more efficiently, and enjoy a comparative advantage. This translates to lower costs and enables our people to enjoy a great variety of products at cheaper prices.

SOCRATES. Indeed. But are there not great differences in wages between civilizations, making neo-slaves more cost effective than, say, your own workers? And does this not result in idle workers in the civilization that is most advanced and has the finest homes and clothes. I detect that the cost of household maintenance will decline with the invasion of cheap goods, but will not wages and employment decline even faster as a prelude to a more impoverished standard of living?

OECONOMIST. It would seem so. But our oeconomists calculate a net gain when we send our traders around the world.

SOCRATES. Your oracles present a most difficult proposition. The United States is the biggest market at all latitudes and longitudes. But your wise men perceive it to be in your best interest to forgo this prime market, allowing neo-slave producers to have it, so you in turn can have the markets where the neo-slaves live. Is that correct?

OECONOMIST. It appears that way.

SOCRATES. Has this net gain indeed come about as promised by your astrologers and wise men?

OECONOMIST. Not exactly. We still have a negative balance of trade and payments.

SOCRATES. This negative balance of which you speak! Is this not an oxymoron? Does not *balance* mean *equity* or *parity*? How, then, can *balance* be negative?

OECONOMIST. "Failure to achieve a balance" might be a better explanation. But this is only temporary. GATT and NAFTA promise more markets. Tourism will bring great benefits to the United States, the Secretary of Commerce has opined.

SOCRATES. These acronym entities, GATT and NAFTA, are they favored by the gods, for if this is not the case, then your people will surely find themselves without employment. And unemployed people cannot purchase the products made available by incoming seamen. And this Cassandra who is Secretary of Commerce, surely no one will believe him if in fact he speaks truth. Therefore, if he is believed, he must be speaking falsehood.

OECONOMIST. We have to be patient.

SOCRATES. Further, it would seem the neo-slaves elsewhere will be unable to buy from your traders simply because they earn too little, being the cheapest producers in trade channels.

OECONOMIST. This was once seen as a problem. However, we now guarantee loans to such nations, in effect providing them with the money needed to buy from the United States.

SOCRATES. Are these loans then repaid in some occult way, for surely even Hermes could not accomplish this impossible task?

OECONOMIST. Well, not generally. The bonds are traded around the world until they become worthless, or the U.S. Treasury satisfies the guarantee, and the taxpayers get the bill.

SOCRATES. Is this procedure not gifting rather than selling? And if citizens must pay taxes to receive cheap goods, does this not negate the concept of comparative advantage the oracle speaks of?

OECONOMIST. Laymen might see it that way, but they lack sophistication in such matters. Actually, corporate profits are enhanced by this trade, and eventually the gross domestic product will reflect a reversal in the balance of trade. The *Fortune* 500 organizations are the most accomplished profit makers in the world, and they will confer their expertise on the American economy.

SOCRATES. But if these *Fortune* 500 organizations rely on largess from the taxed populi, does this not in effect make them relief clients, much like the impoverished and homeless who are maintained by your masters of statecraft? How many new employment opportunities have the *Fortune* 500 wizards created during the past fifteen years?

OECONOMIST. No new jobs have been created in the U.S. As for your *relief client* remark, this has a certain populist appeal among laymen who do not understand trade and the money system. No offense, Socrates, but I am afraid that the philosophers of your age lived in a heavenly city in which truth was absolute.

SOCRATES. If truth is not absolute, then, you seem compelled to accept a debased pragmatism. You seem to rate ideas true if they work, and you also rate them as true if they don't work, but if enough people are confused by them. From what I hear and see, the concept of free international trade seems to have a status of near total acceptance. This seems odd to me, because it violates the single principle on which all oeconomists agree, and that is the principle of the *multiplier*. As I understand it, the principle of the multiplier makes possible the calculation of total national income by furnishing statistics for activity generated as raw materials churn their way through the economy. A bushel of wheat sold into international trade channels delivers only the raw materials value to the farmer and the domestic economy. It misses out on the multiplier it would invoke were all the economic values to be taken out of that bushel of grain. Thus the sale of a bushel of wheat to Sparta at half price would short change Athens (in your case the United States) the amount represented by the parity shortfall as well as the gross domestic income that would have been generated by keeping the full economic cycle at home. Thus I suggest the equation for a bushel of wheat sold at a cheap Spartan half parity price reveals national income missed by half pricing the product in the first place, and by vacating the full multiplier by handing most of the value to the international raw materials buyer or pirate. I have made my computations, Mr. Oeconomist, and now I suggest to you that it takes no master of arithmetic to start the income shortfall countdown. Your national wheat crop at world prices generates only half as much income as it would at an American price. This shortfall cannot churn its way through the economy and obey your state of the arts multiplier. I see that you now roll your eyes like a stricken oxen when I argue these data. Are my abstractions too difficult? Is what I say ambiguous?

OECONOMIST. I would say, O Socrates, that you do not describe the trade situation properly. This isn't the way it works.

SOCRATES. But this is the way it works, and you have the public and private debt to prove it. It would be fatuous to suggest that I am alone in understanding the generation of income. I can't possibly be alone in having made these computations or discerned these truths, so I ask, am I hearing ignorance, or thoroughly informed self interest speaking? In logic, a contradiction is a signal of defeat. The multiplier contradicts everything your GATT and NAFTA have to say—and oeconomists still haven't tried to repeal the law of the multiplier.

OECONOMIST. No. Nevertheless, the absolutes of which you speak are really malleable. The real world is give and take and bargaining, free trade, in short.

SOCRATES. Yes, yes! You forget, we were advanced enough to have discovered the function of pi and Fibonacci's series in my time. I remind you that Eratosthenes was not the first to measure the circumference of this earth, Hipparchus was not the first to understand trigonometry, Pythagoras was not the first to originate that theorem, and Mercator was not the first to create his projection. More important, you Americans were not the first to invent money.

OECONOMIST. No, not money, but you will have to admit that we removed it from its connection with the barbaric metal, gold.

SOCRATES. How clever—and perplexing! I see that your chief piece of money carries a legend affirming that it is a promise to pay the bearer the sum of one dollar. What is this thing, a dollar, of which payment is thus promised?

OECONOMIST. A dollar is the American unit of account, the currency of the realm.

SOCRATES. So there is, I suppose, some concrete object which embodies more firmly that abstract unit of account than does this paper promise? If not gold, wheat or a basket of commodities.

OECONOMIST. There is no such object, O Socrates.

SOCRATES. Indeed? Then what your bank promises is to give the holder of this promise another promise stamped with a different number in case he regards the number stamped on this promise cursed or out of favor with your gods in some way?

OECONOMIST. It would seem indeed to be promising something of that kind. But free trade is honorable.

SOCRATES. I jest. For it is known in my land that the ziggurats, or temples of ancient Babylon, managed by the priests of Baal, conjured up a fraudulent money system similar to yours. It relied on short-changing producers of real wealth, then loaning the wheat producer the wherewithal to put in a new crop. By requiring interest the priests engineered default and bankruptcy. Because there was less money in existence than the amount needed to retire the loans and pay the interest, the growers of wheat had to forfeit their collateral. First the priests of Baal took livestock, then land, then the children of the family were sold into slavery, next the wife, and finally the farmer himself accepted serfdom. I was in your great New York library recently. I was examining papers of one of your Founding Fathers, a Dr. Benjamin Franklin, specifically his *Positions to be Examined Concerning National Wealth*, April 4, 1769. He wrote that there were three ways in which a nation might become wealthy, to wit: /By war, which permits taking by force the wealth of other nations./ By trade, which to be profitable requires cheating. For example [he said] if we give and receive an equal amount of goods and services through trade, there is no profit other than that obtained in our own production cycle./ By agriculture, through which we plant the seeds and create new wealth as if by a miracle. So your defense of free trade is difficult to understand. Anatomically it must be related to the art of war and investing cities for loot to be gained. Surely you will recall how Agamemnon set siege to Troy so that spoils could be added to the Athenian industry, and how the stratagem of the Trojan Horse was used to gain entrance to that city. Our most sacred text, Homer's *Odyssey*, ought to make clear that the trader and the military are one. The pirate preys for loot, as does the businessman, and the triumvirate functions as a sector of the civilization. It employs crafty liars. The supply of lies, much like ignorance, is infinite.

OECONOMIST. But we no longer permit pirates on the high seas, and our exchange relies on comparative advantage, not deception.

SOCRATES. Hold. You forget your own papyrus. In one week I read of several centuries of piracy sanctioned by the Crown of England. In your case, the American Constitution legalizes letters of marque and reprisal.

OECONOMIST. That's old fashioned thinking. Free trade is honorable.

SOCRATES. Is it? Have the requirements for life changed, or do you no longer require food? I told the young man I mentioned that no one can qualify to be a statesman who was totally ignorant of the problems of wheat. Nor is anyone so qualified who allows his country to become dependent on foreign trade for its food supply. It is a law of nations that as populations expand, they will depend on their own raw materials and their own craft production, and less on piracy and business or free trade. When agriculture is allowed to decay, there is concentration on manufacturers. The production of the latter then can't be sold abroad. It would seem that foreign trade, much like reparations, is not an issue of money. Foreign trade, as with two tribesmen exchanging gifts of nature, is basically barter. Thus it appears that the ability to strike a trade balance is annihilated in advance by disparity. A true balance would be much like a pirate leaving payment for loot. Such is not the name of the piracy exercise.

OECONOMIST. I am afraid you over-simplify.

SOCRATES. No. Reason with me for a moment. When mortals came into being, food was already "there"—*there* being the environs where fish could be harvested, meat animals trapped and berries and grains foraged. Every atom of matter—to use our term for the smallest division thereof—acted upon, gleaned, harvested, inhaled, drunk, consumed, fashioned into a home or a statute comes from the very Earth that supports even the gods on Olympus. If you will retreat with me to the very gates of *Hades*, you must admit that earth, air, fire and water have authored the substance on which we live, build, aspire. Unlike the gods (who must exist, otherwise where did the idea come from?), the seats of civilizations have been grafted onto the countryside—in your time as in my own, oeconomist—and on the business of taking food from the hunter, fisherman and peasant producer. But that surplus springs from the Earth, nevertheless, in the first instance. You surmise that I do not comprehend the grammar of the subject. I say that if oeconomics were a science, as you claim, you would not need to defend yourself from criticism either with a conspiracy of silence, or patronizing answers. My dialogue with you is finished. I must turn to an historian so that I can understand how it is that you have chosen what logic tells me is a destructive path. Although I no longer have the life span it would take to read those full shipweights of manuscripts in your book storehouses, I fancy they would tell much the same story. During a short eight year period you now calculate as B.C. 441, the nabobs of privilege turned inward and finally were removed from Athenian office via the mechanism of executions. I know, I face a cup of hemlock myself because of my criticism, but I cannot do otherwise and remain true to myself. I discern that you have your own faceless people who create famines and wars for profit, but you fail to terminate their activity with timely executions. You now have an atmosphere of intimidation afloat, select ridicule of the few who tell the truth, and you hand off to the population an oeconomic plan so absurd, you cannot defend it with a straight face in broad daylight. You pretend that your answers are correct, and you refurbish your pretense with legal decrees based not on lofty ideas, but the first relic of barbarism—war! You worship Ares, the war god, with a fervour never commanded of the lowest peasant in Athens. A child selling lemonade seems to be more schooled in oeconomics than your greatest experts.

OECONOMIST. But we hold, Socrates, that trade is the shining path to peace. If goods do not cross international borders, then armies will. Therefore totally free trade is history's olive branch.

SOCRATES. I marel at your deduction. Yet from your flow of words comes the obvious conclusion that your trade and foreign policy have been a desperate expedient to salvage domestic employment by forcing sales abroad, with armies, of course. Then having shifted unemployment to the neighbor, you cap off this economic device with war to facilitate the consumption of war material. Now you suggest a new

And Now, O Socrates 13

remedy in this seedbed of failure. But you fail to tell your body politic that the real reason their sons and daughters must be sacrificed on foreign killing fields is to synthesize consumption, the required counterpart of production. You scoff at the idea of absolutes. Know by my presence that I have consumed great amounts of literature in your book warehouses. In Athens, we believe in ideas. I now see that others have come and gone who believed in institutions, such as the church. Now, the worse I can discern is that you believe in force, and the best I can say is that you are merely confused. You pretend to rely on institutional power based on this thing you call scientific truth, and yet every facet of your logic is—to borrow one of your own terms—infected with indifference to reality.

In a short note at the end of Scroll #1, there were extended thanks to a young Greek scribe who translated and recorded this dialogue. The name of the oeconomist was lost when bookworms digested the first several wraps of the scroll. The scroll contained no further hint as to how the conversation was made a matter of record.

2.

The dialogue that follows was recorded on magnetic tape at the Library of Congress, Washington, D.C. A transcription and translation was furnished to Socrates by the Greek speaking historian designated in the interview. The historian told Socrates he would have to remain anonymous, or else place his position in jeopardy. This information was not part of the transcript, rather a margin note on the second wrap of Scroll #2.

We can suggest paranoia if we like, nevertheless the information supplied to Socrates reflected thinking at variance with official policy. This policy—circa 1990s—required agencies to exercise drastic measures for control. As Socrates counseled and spoke, a Texas village was invested, not for loot but for venegence, with more Lidice-like victims on the drawing board. It was not a time for candor—or freedom of speech —since officially coercion more than the bribe was being used to control the population. If we read these exchanges correctly, it seems an anonymous historian seized the opportunity to draw upon the past to illustrate the present. As public policy continued to clash with reality, correct thinking took on front burner attention, and servants who stepped outside their role were either dismissed or prosecuted. The first signs of a blind parade toward disintegration were visible, and the historian suggested as much.

THE FOUNDING FATHERS

HISTORIAN. How is it possible, O Socrates, that a scholar of your historical stature would come to a modern scribbler of historical texts for instruction?

SOCRATES. Your craft is a repository of happenings, so surely you have recorded the arcane and the profane. A sovereign state rarely admits its mistakes. This is the reason convulsions routinely savage the lives of most people on Earth. When the rulers seek evidence against its citizens, they are almost always certain to find it. If the sought-for item isn't there when the seekers enter, it will magically appear before they leave. This mindset sees no difficulty legislating family affairs and human rights to accommodate the will of the absconders. For this reason and for these several reasons, I seek the frame of reference that attended the founding of the American nation so that I might know by what convoluted logic you have come to the present impasse.

HISTORIAN. I am only a writer and compiler—and you do me great honor by calling me an historian. As you know, credentials and academic standing cannot confer that title. Only the correct use of logic to ratify facts can entitle one to that distinction. For now it is enough to quote Fisher Ames, one of the ablest men in the American Congress in 1789. He said, "I conceive, sir, that the present Constitution was dictated by commercial necessity more than by any other cause. The want of an efficient government to secure the manufacturing interest, and to advance our commerce, was long seen by men of judgment and pointed out by patriots solicitous to promote our general welfare." The historian Bancroft said, "The necessity for regulating commerce (i.e., for providing a proper tariff) gave the immediate impulse to a more perfect Constitution." The great Daniel Webster, historically known as the great expounder of the Constitution, in a speech at Buffalo, New York in June 1833, declared that "The protection of American labor against the injurious competition of foreign labor, so far at least as respects general handicraft productions, is known historically to have been one end designed to be obtained by establishing the Constitution." It is supreme irony, O Socrates, that the tariff question was the very first subject to be discussed by the First Congress, and for the two hundred plus years of our existence remains the single subject never settled. Nullification, secession, slavery and reconstruction, all have had their times of discussion and have all been forever settled, but the tariff remained a vital question many years later during the Roosevelt administration, and it remains unsettled to this day.

SOCRATES. Then piracy and international business gave your early statesmen the impulse and analysis required to support a protection instrument for government?

HISTORIAN. Absolutely. After all, the threats form England were blatant. And their history was deep seated. I have yet to read an historian who can explain why the industrial revolution came to Europe and England in its trader form. Not even Arnold Toynbee—who invented the term, *industrial revolution*—had an answer. Why didn't it happen in China or your own ancient Greece? Why didn't parenthood for industrialization take place in the Dyak culture of Borneo, or among the Ainu culture of Northern Japan, or even out among the Adaman islanders? I can suggest an answer, but I need your assistance to determine whether it is correct.

SOCRATES. Philosophy has to lead. We know of man's acquisitive nature, and I dare say I can factor it into our discourse. This industrial revolution, it must have responded to a special philosophy not available among the civilizations you mentioned, including my own.

HISTORIAN. Yes, Socrates. Let me tell you of a mythology that remained afloat to the effect that Columbus proved the world was as round as the Sun. You know this is false. Your learned men knew the Earth was a sphere long before our medieval mapmakers surmised as much. Your own Plato spoke of the Pyramids of Egypt, of Atlantis and Lemura. But it was not until Magellan circumnavigated the globe that rulers discerned the Earth was finite, its resources limited. Queen Elizabeth founded the East India Company for the purpose of plundering the planet in A.D. 1600. England elevated herself above all others on Earth based on John Locke's philosophy called "right of conquest."

SOCRATES. How is this different from our Greek wars and the right to loot?

HISTORIAN. Forgive me, Socrates, but your civilization collapsed in harmony with Oswald Spengler's 2,000 year cycle. Rome and Carthage collapsed. England entered her spring and summer, before she too started her long decline. At this point in time the American nation was founded, during the late 16th Century, these philosophies dovetailed to become one for England, and a counterveiling one for America.

SOCRATES. Please continue. I sense that these philosophical leanings are more important to my inquiry than all the notes you have concerning commerce, philosophy—however debased—being the father, commerce being the mother of history.

HISTORIAN. You anticipate my discourse, O Socrates. Sir, the East India Company founded Haileybury College in England for the purpose of staffing its quest for empire. It trained soldiers, businessmen and religious folk to serve the East India Company. Within two hundred years, Haileybury College was called upon to inventory the planet and its resources. The man in charge was the head of Haileybury's Department of Economics, one Thomas Robert Maltus, philosopher, a minister of the Christian gospel.

SOCRATES. And what was his philosophy?

HISTORIAN. Maltus had a population theory. It was based on the idea that the finite planet would soon be overtaxed by new life. This new life, he held, was expanding geometrically, whereas the food supply gained new efficiency only on an arithmetical basis. Therefore some life was superfluous. Malthus was soon joined by one Charles Darwin, who argued the survival of the fittest. In the minds of these philosophers, God threw the dice, and the fittest had a divine right to survive, prosper and multiply. This is the philosophy you seek, my dear Socrates. It is the philosophy that set the Dutch, French, Spanish, finally the English, on a course of conquest until each coveted every acre, every sandbar, every spit of land on Earth. Finally the English pronounced expendable any population they could bully. Outside of continental wars, the British rarely fought an enemy that wore shoes—except the American colonies, of course.

SOCRATES. And the American colonies wouldn't bully, as you put it.

HISTORIAN. No. But the British tried. In 1699 the English Parliament decreed that "after the first day of December, no wool, yarn, cloth or woollen manufacturers of the English plantations in America shall be shipped from any of said plantations, or otherwise laden, in order to be transported thence to any place whatsoever, under a penalty of forfeiting both ship and cargo, and $500 for each offense." It was the goal of a few international traders of Great Britain to manufacture for the entire world, and to monopolize most reproductive power—and, as one historian put it—"to keep all other countries in a state of industrial vassalage."

The Founding Fathers 19

SOCRATES. Would it be correct to say this was accomplished with a greater storehouse of goods in the hands of traders, cheap labor, and the merchant and military marine, as well as pirates under letters of marque, and with warriors? Surely such a debased "philosophy" could not prevail on its own merits?

HISTORIAN. Precisely. The public policy emanated from the top of the political spectrum. Documentation for this statement is impeccable. Lord Brougham, in 1816, told the House of Commons, "It is well worth while to incur a loss upon the first exportation, in order, by the glut, to stifle in the cradle those infant manufacturers in the United States, which the war has forced into existence."

SOCRATES. To ignore such an ominous statement would be much like ignoring Sparta's on-going military buildup. So your men of wisdom drew up a Constitution to protect citizens from a grasping commercial power.

HISTORIAN. Yes. We call these men Founding Fathers. They directed the Revolutionary War, of course, and they tried to direct the peace via the status quo. O Socrates, be patient. Let me read to you what a contemporary, George Mason, had to say. "And so the years from 1783 to 1789 were lovely, halcyon days for the merchants and statesmen of Great Britain. In about three years' time, nearly all the money of the country had passed into the pockets of British merchants and manufacturers, and we were left poor indeed; for not only did they take from us our money, but they took, also, our good name for integrity, independence and common-sense, which we had won in the Revolutionary War. As there was no tariff to prevent it, foreign nations literally poured in upon us their products of every kind and description in such quantities, and at such prices, that our people could not compete with them. Our domestic industries were suspended. The weaver, the shoemaker, the hatter, the saddler, the rope-maker, and many others, were reduced to bankruptcy; our markets were glutted with foreign products; prices fell; our manufacturers, generally, were ruined; our laborers beggared; our artisans without employment; our merchants insolvent, and our farmers necessarily followed all these classes into the vortex of general financial destruction. Depreciation seized upon every species of property. Legal pressure to enforce payment of debts caused alarming sacrifices of both personal and real-estate; spread distress far and wide among the masses of the people; aroused in the hearts of the sufferers the bitterest feelings against lawyers, the courts and the whole creditor class; led to a popular clamor for stay-laws and various other radical measures of supposed relief, and finally filled the whole land with excitement, apprehension and sense of weakness and a tendency to despair of the Republic. Inability to pay even necessary taxes became general, and often these could be collected only by levy and sale of the homestead." You asked about free trade, O Socrates, and now I give you free trade. In Massachusetts, fully a third of the people joined Shay's Rebellion because of the poverty and distress visited on them by free trade. In sparsely populated Connecticut, some five hundred farms were seized to taxes, the owners being too poor to pay, and the situation was hardly better in the rest of New England. There was no market for real estate. Debtors were compelled to sell their land. They were ruined. Men distrusted each other. The historian Mason wrote, "Had there been no free trade, there would have been no inundation of foreign goods, there would have been no drain of specie; had there been no drain of specie, there would have been no lack of circulating medium; had there been no such distress, there would have been no insubordination to the state."

SOCRATES. Yes, yes! The portrait seems clear. Ruin came to your Founding Fathers, free trade being the distributor of general malaise. Unchallenged free trade managed by the foreigner was followed rather quickly by imports in excess of exports—"failure to achieve a balance of trade," your oeconomist told me. This glut of production from foreign climes forced suspension of your own manufacturing enterprises, followed by a loss of specie and the necessary stoppage of almost all business. Without business and domestic trade, laborers and artisans fell idle. Without earnings and with the existence of universal debt, property declined in value and became worthless. General distress and ruin became the legacy of all, for which reason your then young nation endured rebellions such as the Shay affair. Was this the closest approach to free trade ever tried? If so you have a fair indication of the dangers and calamities to be harvested. Tell me, by what magic was your guiding oracle able to convince your countrymen that free trade was a false, if speculative idea?

HISTORIAN. Over a span of nearly two hundred years, agriculture has been a precursor, going into or emerging from depression. I refer you—only as a sample, mind you— to Robert J. Walker of Mississippi, the Secretary of Treasury during the Polk administration. The South under slavery was dedicated to free trade. Cotton was king. Listen to this man. "We have more fertile lands than any other nation. We can raise a greater variety of products, and, it may be said, could feed and clothe the people of nearly all the world. Agriculture is our chief employment. It is best adapted to our situation. We can raise a larger surplus of agricultural products, and a greater variety than almost any other nation, and at cheaper rates. Remove then from agriculture all our restrictions, and by its own unfettered power it will break down all foreign restrictions, and, ours being removed, would feed the hungry and clothe the poor of our fellowmen, through all the densely peopled nations of the world." Ezra Taft Benson and Earl Butz as Secretaries of Agriculture continued to echo this conceit in our own time, and often they are believed by those less endowed with mental acuity.

SOCRATES. Conjectural politics and conjectural economics seem to be the curse of the simple minded, or the boast of the dishonest—or, perhaps, the banner of the opportunist. In Athens we endured no less than three captures of the government by militants disposed as you have described. In each case the seizure was accompanied by attempts to secure perpetual revenue independent of a further expenditure of energy by the daring few. In one instance approximately one hundred thirty were executed for bending the welfare of all to their own designs. Were there any mass executions when your Founding Fathers constructed a government to protect the American citizens?

HISTORIAN. None, O Socrates.

SOCRATES. That is remarkable. But the free trade interlude ended, did it not? And your nation recaptured the values that prompted the founding of the United States in the first place. I have been told about communism, and how it was rejected by your people, yet promoted for the Asian land mass by your leaders.

HISTORIAN. It is true, at one time communism seemed to be the answer for the great minds at Cambridge, Lord John

Maynard Keynes included. Yet by the time Josef Stalin took command of the U.S.S.R., the highest inner circles knew communism to be a failure. Aleksandr Solzhenitsyn related this intelligence in volume two of his *Gulag Archipeligo*. He also explained that Stalin closeted himself for several days with a Turkish businessman named Naftaly A. Frenkel, an old friend. Frenkel reasoned, as do most businessmen, that values and profits are predatory, always achieved at the expense of others. He told Stalin that in order for communism to succeed, it would be necessary to get free labor. This conclusion achieved, the two then proceeded to construct their syllogism. Frenkel pointed out that not just any labor would do. This free labor had to know how to do things—and thus the judgment was made to draw up a list of engineers. *Now*, said Frenkel, *arrest every seventh one!* These workers would bring their own energy into the system. And the system would harvest this energy, giving all those who confessed to choreographed crimes only thin cabbage soup and minimal support for life. Most would be dead in a year or two. This free labor built and staffed the Gulag. As the Gulag expanded, coal minerals, gold—especially gold—and timber met the raw materials requirements of what pundits called "the future now." There was a problem with this business equation. It did not answer the requirements of economics. Because free labor was used, raw materials failed to generate the base income that could—via the multiplier—hoist up the national income. As a consequence the Soviet economy always operated without an adequate social surplus, or a proper profit for the system. Cheap labor in fact sounded the death knell for communism that far back. It was only a decade or two before the Stalin era that Henry Ford reasoned, *If we do not raise the industrial wage to fifty cents an hour, the worker will never be able to own a Model T car*, our motorized chariot. Accordingly, Ford took the lead in raising the American industrial wage to fifty cents an hour. Others accepted this reasoning and joined the effort. On this basis the United States built the biggest steel industry, the biggest auto industry, the biggest just-about-everything. There were depressions called panics, and then there came that engineered depression of the 1930s, which was crafted by business people who wanted the disparity required by free trade. There were also periods of structural balance. These were created by stabilization measures, by raw materials prices in line with wages and capital costs, and by an understanding that free labor was a delusion of maximum dimension because the absence of income short-circuits the exchange equation. Today, half the world is coming apart because the act of production is not creating and distributing the credits needed for consumption. It took over seven decades for Stalin's economic error to undo communism. And yet the U.S. is following Frenkel's advice in its own dumb way. According to many Congressmen and an incumbent President, the United States too needs free labor—or at the bare minimum, cheap labor. A rationale for this Stalinesque conclusion has now arrived in the public prints: a free trade agreement with Mexico to lessen "pressure on workers to cross the Rio Grande in search of work in the United States."

SOCRATES. These arguments you cite seem as thin as a garment of cloth from Gaza. I am astounded by what you tell me, and I must have proof. I must see the archives and examine more documentation, both in order to understand the unique brand of leadership exercised by the Founding Fathers, and the marble-like density between the ears of your present leaders. They must. . .

The Scroll was too deteriorated for further recovery of its con-

tents. Scholars have speculated on what might have followed "They must," but the fragment was too short for meaningful extension without undue speculation. A likely explanation is that the historian simply ran out of tape and handed an incomplete manuscript to Socrates. Also, the transcription might have recorded something to identify the Library of Congress worker, and was removed because Socrates was being monitored by the intelligence community. Socrates knew as much. Accordingly, he hid his manuscripts with confederates who sought him out and questioned him endlessly. In general the press ignored Socrates. Computer searches of The Washington Post and The New York Times revealed not one mention of Socrates in America during the period covered by The Lost Dialogues. Only one item, a short article in The Street Corner, a Greenwich Village tabloid, surfaced while this compilation was in process.

SOC HITS HARD

On the street he has the mein of an eccentric, yet crowds form up whenever he speaks. He identifies himself as Socrates of Athens. He walks the blazing streets of the village barefooted, always wearing a freshly laundered white Greek jumpsuit.

His topic is virtue. He enjoys deflating windbags in government. In this city, where prophets and oracles are plentiful, and the ability to think is at low tide, old Soc stimulates. He finds answers to all our pressing problems. Unfortunately, the problems continue to be propounded as though solutions had never been found.

The rest of the newspaper article was chewed into oblivion by mice.

3.

*We cannot know why Socrates sought out an archivist sudden-
ly and without provocation. Certainly the historian told him what
he wanted to know. We can assume Socrates was familiar with the
grammar of the subject. His questions and his answers to questions
reveal a surprising rapport with modern ideas which—on second
examiniation—were really ancient ideas. The tall buildings, the
escalators and elevators, the tramways, the airplanes and sub-
marines were merely modern claptrap to Socrates. Perhaps he
turned to the archieves because he wanted to close the gap between
the modern age and his own. There he could see drafts, indictments,
instruments of government, acts in their legislated form, documents not greatly different from those used in his own society. The
first line recovered from Scroll #3 has Socrates speaking. Scholars
believe this Scroll was developed from notes. Brackets imply ex-
traneous comments by the translating scribe.*

THE PIRATE-MILITARY COMPLEX

SOCRATES. I have been told about certain Founding Fathers
and leaders who successfully set out to protect the
American nation from the pirate-military-business complex
that prowls the sea. Who were these wise men and what did
they say that convinced one and all to protect farms and
industry from import invasion and from alien usurpers?
What documents are there to link history with reality?

ARCHIVIST. The first significant act of the First Congress
established a protective tariff. This law was signed by
Founding Father George Washington on July 4, 1789. I have
here the original. You can view, but not touch this document. It is sealed in a controlled atmosphere.

SOCRATES. I see. May I presume that fabricators and career politicos had by then seized the government so they could write legislation most favorable to their interests?

ARCHIVIST. By no means, O Socrates. The great majority of the First Congress were farmers. They lived close to the soil, and therefore close to reality.

SOCRATES. Then they must have rejected the calculations associated with the Robert J. Walker and Earl Butz types, that your peasant-farmers could feed the world, which I perceive to be a Herculean task. Indeed, extended to other pursuits, such a calculation would suggest that your small population—which, as I visit, is no more than 6% of the total world population—can wet nurse the world, fight its wars, keep it on a dole, supply a military-business, pirate complex to regulate affairs, and do it with an exchange that consistently fails to achieve balance. I digress. Tell me more about the Founding Fathers.

ARCHIVIST. No less than five of the Founding Fathers became presidents while the protective tariff of 1789 was anchored in the statute books.

SOCRATES. Indeed. And what were their documented pronouncements?

ARCHIVIST. George Washington spoke of the free people he led. "Their safety and interest require that they promote such manufactures as tend to render them independent of other for essentials, particularly military supplies." During his eighth year as president, Washington reiterated the proposition that it was the business of the nation to protect the producers who generated income for the nation. John Adams, Thomas Jefferson, James Madison, James Monroe, none found a hint of dissatisfaction with protection. No one suggested repeal of the law.

[At this point there were disjointed notes in the manuscript, probably because Socrates was scrutinizing several documents associated with the first five presidents. These notes merely suggested the identities of the several documents on display.]

SOCRATES. I have heard breath-taking dialogue concerning Shay's Rebellion. Did the Act of which you speak smile more favorably on your people?

ARCHIVIST. The archives of the nation suggest as much. A history of the era reads as follows. [An original was handed to Socrates while the archivist read.] "Agriculture became more extensive and prosperous. Commerce increased with wonderful rapidity. Old industries were revived, and many new ones were established in all parts of the country. Our merchant-navy was revived and multiplied. All branches of domestic trade were prosperous. Our revenue soon became sufficient to pay the expenses of the government, and give relief to its creditors. The people again became contented and industrious. And the whole country seemed to be, and was, on the high road to great national wealth and prosperity." No changes in the law of 1789 were enacted until 1812, and the general prosperity continued through that period.

SOCRATES. In your year 1812, why did not your men of wisdom somehow enshrine this law into the more permanent Constitution—for they must not have, else I would not read in your daily tocsin about so much distress being visited on your fellowpersons—excuse me, I find it awkward that your nouns do not have gender, and these

The Pirate-Military Complex 29

coined words such as fellowpersons instead of fellowmen and womanager instead of manager are equally awkward.

ARCHIVIST. I apologize for the illiteracy of the hour. Many people do not understand that the term *man* has as its primary meaning *Homo sapien*, and does not refer to sex. To answer your question, it is indeed difficult to explain the 1812-1816 shift to free trade under the Democratic Party. It may be that Thomas Jefferson best captured the design and danger ever present in the Republic. Thomas Jefferson identified the source that was ever willing to undo American prosperity, namely the banking interests. "I believe," he wrote, "that banking institutions are more dangerous than standing armies. Already they have raised up a monied aristocracy that has set the government at defiance." These institutions were able to convince the people, already prosperous, they could increase their comfort by buying cheap from the foreigner.

SOCRATES. Prosperity leads to greed. And greed undoes prosperity by undercutting its source. This has been the course even in my clime. It promises freedom but delivers chains, the often penalty for a lack of virtue. This promise that free trade will make comforts available to the poor seems to—by sleight of hand—increase the number of poor rather than make tolerable their burden. Pray tell, this annihilation of protection must have been relieved, else your nation would not have achieved some of the comforts I discern.

ARCHIVIST. In the year of the common era, 1824, the general tariff was restored, as was prosperity. In 1832, President Andrew Jackson declared the state of the union excellent. After eight years of protection, he said, "Our country presents on every side, marks of prosperity and happiness, unequalled, perhaps, in any other portion of the world." Here is that recorded speech. Henry Clay said of that era, "On a general survey we behold cultivation extended; the arts flourishing; the face of the country improved; our people fully and profitably employed; the public countenance exhibiting tranquility, contentment and happiness; its public debt of two wars nearly redeemed; and, to crown all, the public treasury overflowing. If the term of seven years were to be selected of the greatest prosperity which this people has enjoyed since the establishment of their present Constitution, it would be exactly that period of seven years which immediately followed the passage of the Tariff of 1824."

[Socrates paused for an hour to study the related documents.]

SOCRATES. Do your archives contain the debates that attended your decline and fall?

ARCHIVIST. Our archieves are complete. From the age of Jackson to the terms of Woodrow Wilson, it was always a case of the South linking arms with northern bankers to lower tariff protection and promote free trade. In 1833, free trade prevailed again.

SOCRATES. May I surmise that the promised goods and services became less available than ever, and that the promised international division of labor did not result in more jobs being created among nations supportive of traders? Did this Act of 1833 then cause the warehousers of specie and gold to achieve prosperity?

ARCHIVIST. The archives tell us that a new word entered the

The Pirate-Military Complex 31

common vocabulary: *panic*.

SOCRATES. Your rulers have their tenure in office terminated or extended every two, four and six years. Can you tell me how the battle went with this single issue, protection, that remains unresolved to this day?

ARCHIVIST. Protection returned once more in 1842, common era. The archive keepers recorded that immediately financial gloom disappeared. Business revived. There was full employment, and therefore an improved market. This prosperity included the farm. In 1844, the Democratic National Convention again endorsed free trade, and nominated James K. Polk for president. Duplicity reigned supreme in that election, and with it free trade surfaced as a victor again. Polk's campaign rhetoric involved elusive sayings. Once the election was over, the real meaning came clear—a free trade scenario became law through mendacity.

SOCRATES. I think I understand. Since my arrival—by reading the news—I have encountered curious terms such as *global village*, and I have read tomes that pretend to assign a loss of freedom to protection, when it is clear to all but the simple-minded that without economic freedom born of an ability to earn, these other expressions are sophistry of the worst sort. Surely your people have the mental acuity to hear what is said.

ARCHIVIST. It would seem so. Not many people could win a debate with Daniel Webster, for instance. Our archives have the speech he made over three days running, July 25, 27 and 28, 1846. If you will permit an abstract thereof, O Socrates, I could summarize.

SOCRATES. Surely, proceed. But allow me to see the document.

ARCHIVIST. Daniel Webster said, "You indulge in the luxury of taxing the poor man and the laborer! That is the whole tendency, the whole character, the whole effect of the bill. One may see everywhere in it the desire to revel in the delight of taking away men's employment. It is not a bill for the people or the masses. It is not a bill to add to the comforts of those in middle life, or of the poor. It is not a bill for employment. It is a bill for the relief of the highest and most luxurious classes of the country, and a bill imposing onerous duties on the great industrious masses, and for taking away the means of living from labor everywhere throughout the land." He showed clearly that this bill narrowed and diminished our industries, and thus deprived the masses of needed employment, and added: "The interest of every laboring community requires diversity of occupations, pursuits, and objects of industry. The more that diversity is multiplied, even extended, the better. To diversify employment is to increase employment and to enhance wages. And, sir, take this great truth; place it on the title-page of every book of political economy intended for the use of the United States; put it in every *Farmers' Almanac*; let it be the heading of the column of every *Mechanics' Magazine*; proclaim it everywhere, and make it a proverb, that where there is work for the hands of men, there will be work for their teeth. Where there is employment there will be bread. It is a great blessing to the poor to have cheap food, but greater than that, prior to that and of still higher value, is the blessing of being able to buy food by honest and respectable employment. Employment feeds and clothes and instructs. Employment gives health, sobriety and morals. Constant employment and well-paid labor produce, in a country like ours, general prosperity, content, and cheerfulness." The leading newspapers worked very hard to prevent its passage, but in vain. Debate did not seem to matter. The same tired argument about feeding the world and driving foreign industry to the wall with greater skills and better technology—the slave argument, meaning cheaper labor—prevailed. The Robert J. Walker argument prevailed.

SOCRATES. The same results?

ARCHIVIST. The same results, albeit a bit postponed by the Mexican War, California gold, and world problems such as famine in Ireland, European revolutions and the Crimean War. It's all in the archives. In 1857, common era, it was lower tariffs again, and a deeper depression. James Buchanan, the last President before the Civil War, spoke with surprising candor about the effects of free trade. Lincoln, of course, came to grips with the real issue, free labor, or slavery. The free trade war brought on by the South was inevitable. The 1860 Democratic National Convention reiterated its free trade pledge as platform fare. It mattered not. The fourth protection period—1861 to 1891—was off and running. Textbooks nowadays teach children about the Civil War in a patronizing way so as not to offend sensibilities. However the archives say that only two objectives were boldly proclaimed by the South—a government the cornerstone of which was slavery, and an economic system based on free trade around the world. With a slave labor force, this may have made sense. With a free labor force, this was unacceptable.

SOCRATES. I gather from your remarks that the opposing forces—free trade vs. protection—in fact compromised their positions under your Woodrow Wilson administration.

ARCHIVIST. I am sorry, I cannot discuss the Wilson era. I am a specialist in documents up to and through the Taft administration. To engage you in a dialogue focused on the great schoolman would be to overstep my academic role, my credentials and standing. The country is full of people who would attack and eliminate the Federal Reserve. This is a subject no scholar will discuss in the United States. It is one no legislator will even pretend to understand. Sir, my personal security depends on my anonymity. Please, never quote me. To proceed further you will have to examine the money creation issue, and I cannot assist in this.

SOCRATES. Pardon me, but do I detect a trembler? It has never been my nature to grovel. Nevertheless I will honor your wish for anonimity. I am puzzled, for it clear to me that your archieves—with documents enough to satisfy anyone—suggest that your own Founding Fathers considered land as the basis for national wealth, and this national policy seems to have continued into the century of my visit, at least to 1913 when the Federal Reserve was created.

ARCHIEVIST. You will excuse me, I hope, when I tell you the Federal Reserve System established national banking to bring uniformity into the financial system. It gave us currency not related to the land, its wealth and potential.

SOCRATES. I am confused. Your oeconomist told me the currency was backed by more currency within the banking chain and with no relationship to lasting natural wealth. I see this as repudiation of a reasoned system extending in an unbroken line all the way back to before the Penelopean wars in what you call ancient Greek city-states. I will excuse you and I will find someone in the money warehousing craft to answer my question. Surely your Woodrow Wilson authored some curious innovations to deal with coin of the realm?

ARCHIVIST. Indeed, he did. Unravel the money issue and you will answer the economic paradox. But no banker will help you. No lawmaker will smile on your quest. Lincoln money. . .

The last two words of a sentence, cut short, may have been a note to the effect that Socrates wanted to see something on the greenbacks of the Lincoln era, but this is not certain. Half a hundred other notes along the edges of the scrolls could not be read because of insect damage. Of all the scrolls, #3 remains the most enigmatic and disjointed. In fact the dialogue appears to have been constructed from notes and documents, rather than a transcription of continuing conversation. Socrates never again allowed his awl-sharp questions to be compromised, as the next section amply illustrates.

4.

Although Socrates vowed to examine a banker, it does not appear that he could gain an audience. This must have been arrogance raised to power figures, as far as Socrates was concerned. Citizens came to him for the measures of wisdom they sought, and to have a common operator of a money warehouse issue a snub must have set up in the Greek philosopher a great wonderment. Still, there were questions the oeconomist hadn't answered, and the archievist wouldn't even consider. We know Socrates had a guide, for he set out to interview a man of small means, an essentric who often preached to tourists and locals in Washington Square, Greenwich Village, New York. His dias was the soapbox, his topic esoteric empathy. Only one topic could cause him to forgo a regular speech and settle down to trade in intelligence. The man, Socrates, believed had achieved virtue.

PERSEPHONE'S FOOTFALLS

SOCRATES. I must know why the mere mention of the Federal Reserve strikes terror in the hearts of academics, common citizens, government workers, as though the topic was too sacred to be handled in debate or lesser discourse. I have already examined an oeconomist regarding the dollar, which I was told was a unit of account. I was also told that there was no object which embodies more firmly the abstract unit of account than did this paper promise. I may point out, with the support of logic, that money is an outgrowth of barter, and that exchange could be accomplished with all types of money, that is, a common denominator commodity. Chicken feathers can't be used for money; they are too plentiful. Paper notes won't serve, for their appearance depends on honesty in government. If Diogenes could not find an honest man in all Greece, what chance have we? We settled for gold because its arrival after discovery seemed to match the population growth and the tempo of goods crafted as the population matured. How did your wonderful country operate before the arrival of this behemoth, the Federal Reserve?

ECCENTRIC. O Socrates, I am the least of scholars, a vagabond of the streets, tolerated and dispised. Why would you take seriously my ranting. I am a diversion for the witless mob. If they could reason, my jawbone would slay more Phillistines than Sampson slew with the jawbone of that unheralded ass. But alas and alack, they cannot reason and therefore I cannot convince. So why me, Socrates?

SOCRATES. I see virtue oozing out of every pore in your face, old man. And you must know that I can reason, so tell me, what kind of a money system did your America have, and how did you manage to hold off the commercial pirates so dedicated to the ruin of others? Your Founding Fathers must have been uncommonly brilliant to have achieved even a measure of stability without enough gold. And after your War for Southern Secession, you expanded. How?

ECCENTRIC. When this nation's economy boomed after the Civil War until World War I, the markets developed a system to meet the needs for effecting in a non-inflationary way the growth process. The basic principle of sound commercial banking evolved in free domestic markets. The gold exchange values of things produced coming into the markets were briefly monetized, as though they were so much gold, by the commercial lending process, which involved automatically self-liquidating short-term loans. When the loans were made, the banks created corresponding credits to the checking accounts of the shippers, amounts not deducted from other checking accounts. In effect this made the gold standard flexible enough so that the great unforeseen increase in production and even greater need for transactions money was accommodated. These newly created purchasing media were cancelled by repayment of the loans as things were sold in the market. No economist invented the system. No governments created it. Human beings operating in free domestic markets coped with problems for which no solution previously had been provided.

SOCRATES. Then you consider the production and sale of raw materials—products from the soil—as money, literally, as an earned dollar?

ECCENTRIC. Yes. Of course that would be rational and therefore displeasing to those who want something for nothing. That is why governments reserve for themselves the right to issue money, which leads to inflation because of the inherent dishonesty of officials. You asked about the Federal Reserve. It offends reason because it constructs a credit device that leads to bankruptcy. It dissipates the savings and future earnings of the people. The process of creating wealth starts with the production of raw materials, namely products of the planet itself. Manufacturing, transportation, and other functions of business and capital represent only services which could not be performed at all if raw materials were not first produced.

SOCRATES. In my land, citizens allow nothing other than gold as an exchange medium. How has it come about that a mere parchment is accepted when it is no longer a receipt for that common denominator commodity, gold?

ECCENTRIC. The present money system evolved in the wake of the establishment of the Federal Reserve System. This took place during the Wilson administration so that banking could better accommodate free international trade, the linchpin of Wilson's fourteen points. I suppose the idea was inspired by Mayer Anselm Rothschild's dictum, *Permit me to issue and control the money of a nation, and I care not who makes its laws.*

SOCRATES. Surely your Founding Fathers understood the nature of money, that it first came from the Earth as raw production, then grew out of barter exchange?

ECCENTRIC. Our presidents, starting with Washington, ending with Wilson, understood this generally. For this reason, in spite of depressions and wars, a market basket of goods averaged the same in price in 1913 as it had one hundred years earlier. Our second President, John Adams, put the situation in perspective. "All the perplexities, confusion, and distress in America arise not from defeats in the situation of confederation, not from want of honor or virtue, so much as from downright ignorance of the nature of coin, credit and circulation."

SOCRATES. Indeed, much of that ignorance must be my own, for I confess I do not comprehend the strange rules that seem to attend creation of your money. I can comprehend that a government can issue promises, but I understand in your system you confer this largess on your Federal Reserve System, a private banking system. How does the Federal Reserve get the money to buy government securities?

ECCENTRIC. The Fed creates it.

SOCRATES. Out of what?

ECCENTRIC. Out of the right to issue credit money. Dissidents such as President James A. Garfield put this penchant into unequivocal terms—"Whoever controls the volume of money in any country is absolute master of all industry and commerce."

SOCRATES. I see. And I discern that the history of your country—in terms of a common denominator—has been one of tariffs in, tariffs out, each free international trade era followed by distress and a return to protection for basic industries and agriculture. But I discern that something quite basic happened during the Wilson administration. Please enlighten me?

ECCENTRIC. Using every art of persuasion, the schoolman President was able to choreograph the passage of no less than four measures that in effect undid the Constitution, establishment of the Federal Reserve being one of them. Once this money power was enthroned, the rich and famous were assured relative immunity form a second measure, the tax on income.

SOCRATES. And what was that mechanism?

ECCENTRIC. It was a law setting up Foundations for protecting the wealthy. More important, the income tax made it easy to dismiss the tariffs collected as necessary income for government operations. Now free international trade could proceed without even that minimal disturbance. Few people comprehend the connection.

SOCRATES. You mentioned that there were four accomplishments, if you will excuse the term?

ECCENTRIC. Yes. Under the U.S. Constitution all treaties

required Senate ratification. Wilson's fourth accomplishment was emasculation of state political power by requiring a common vote to elect Senators. Previously, Senators had been elected by state legislators acting as representatives in a Republic The clarion call was for democracy—I call it mob-ocracy. The change was subtle, and it contributed to a changed attitude toward free international trade over a period of time. I hope it has been explained to you, O Socrates, that the population rejected Wilson's ideas, especially some of his fourteen points that had to do with shipments on the high seas and free trade.

SOCRATES. Yes, this has come to my attention, as have trade wars between my own era and your present. I am curious, how did President Lincoln, who dismissed slavery, see the role of the money power? There was money power even during the Civil War struggle, was there not?

ECCENTRIC. Lincoln said, "The money power preys upon the nation in times of peace, and conspires against it in times of adversity. It is more despotic than monarchy, more insolent than autocracy, more selfish than bureaucracy. It denounces, as public enemies, all who question its methods or throw light upon its crimes."

SOCRATES. Did the Federal Reserve worsen the situation? I discern that the freed black slaves continued to be oppressed, and that the whole of the working population was reduced to a condition of serfdom. I have spoken with an oeconomist who wanted me to rhapsodize, "Only in America." I took this to mean that boasts of noble deeds were in order, but I now learn of an iniquitous money system through which oppression has become refined, yet remains no less cruel than the old system of chattel slavery.

ECCENTRIC. That may be, but it must be remembered, Socrates, that American industrialists were disinterested in pursuing foreign markets during the years after Wilson *because* employment and production—industrial and agricultural—generated the needed income to consume the domestic production. Unfortunately, free international trade beckoned the unwary, and mesmerized politicians who were rapidly losing touch with the voice of the people.

SOCRATES. How so?

ECCENTRIC. Congress passed the McNary-Haugen bills twice, and President Calvin Coolidge vetoed them twice. These measures sought to protect American farmers from the cheap labor of backwards parts of the world. Congress sheltered American industry behind the Fordney-Mc-Cumber Tariff. Even though there was farm distress at the end of the Great War, the nation endured and constructed prosperity up to and through the 1920s.

SOCRATES. Did the people again reject protection? Did they again seek cheap foreign goods?

ECCENTRIC. No. As Charles A. Lindberg Sr. pointed out, the Federal Reserve was used to create a panic scientifically. In fact, the panic or depression was the first scientifically created one in American history. It was manufactured much as one would create and compute a mathematical problem. Years after the crash, pundits assigned blame for the crash to the Smoot-HawleyTariff Act which even considered for half a year after the start of the panic.

SOCRATES. I am afraid I will have to require documentation for this fantastic statement. It revolts me and it would revolt the gods on Olympus, I am certain.

ECCENTRIC. I respect your prudence. Come with me to my pad. I will exhibit to you, and then quote from *The History of Money in the United States,* by attorney Willis A. Overholser. [There was unrecorded conversation during the short walk. Once in the eccentric's pad, the old street talker read to Socrates as follows:] "One of the most devastating manipulations of the Federal Reserve System occurred during the year 1920. On May 18, 1920, the Federal Reserve Board and the Federal Advisory Council met in Washington, D.C., at which time resolutions were passed, ordering the pursuance of a drastic policy of deflation for the avowed purpose of reducing prices and wages so that American citizens could no longer even approximately consume their own production, and producers were thus compelled to hunt the rest of the world looking for markets." The Great Depression foamed up in the wake of this tryst with so-called free international trade. [It appears that Socrates and the eccentric talked for some time. At this point in the scroll we learn that a large band recorder captured the conversation for later retrieval. The next part of the scroll is clear enough.] Here, let me turn toward my spy. [Spy seems to be the pet name the Greenwich Village essentric called a small voice activated recorder.]

SOCRATES. This trading system seems to have produced terrible unemployment. And—as these dialogues have revealed—a negative balance of trade and payments seems flawed, and certainly the money system appears to be too mysterious for most mortal intellects. I read in your papyrus that hundreds, even thousands of banks are troubled or insolvent, and it seems that not one can comply with the double-entry accounting system created by your monks and which are enforced on other businesses. Are you not fearful of the curse of Demeter?

ECCENTRIC. I have no bankable funds, and had I such I would not entrust them to institutions so completely bankrupt. Demeter—yes, I know the curse under its Roman name, Ceres, the goddess of harvest wealth.

SOCRATES. Demeter cursed Erysichthon so that no abundance could satisfy him. He was sentenced to starve in the act of devouring food. Finally, he consumed himself. Your system seems to have been so cursed. And yet I am told it has functioned so far?

ECCENTRIC. Ever since the Roosevelt administration, thank you Socrates.

SOCRATES. That would be, I suppose, not because of the rather strange rules of which you have told me, but because they are administered by men of great ability and wisdom, oracles so far-seeing they can override the simple and obvious system of your Founding Fathers.

ECCENTRIC. It would seem that that must be the reason, rather than the rules themselves, O Socrates.

SOCRATES. This leaves me with a troublesome question. Your laws and constabularies seem to proscribe the possession of too many dollar units. In order to be a sterling citizen, it seems a person must prove he or she has stones in the head, and has placed for safekeeping all dollars in institutions that are technically insolvent. Is it rational to demand or comply with such a cancellation of personal freedom?

ECCENTRIC. This is being done by modern Jannissaries "for each citizen's own protection," O Socrates. I do not approve. We know the source of wealth, that is why we worship

Persephone, you and I, the radiant maiden of spring and summer. Listen Socrates! Can you not hear Persephone's footfalls?

SOCRATES. Old man—I call you old, yet I must have seen many winters before you saw one, I hear! And I tear off my winter garments of repentence when I see the season of the flowers arrive. But have you seen that there is nothing new under the Sun? Your Federal Reserve uses the magician's sleight of hand to baffle the fools and fool the wise, to use the words of a poet. I marvel that your pundits look down on those you call ancients, and yet you crawl in your own primeval slime and live in fear of a myth created not in some heavenly Olympus, but by the least of mortals, the crafty and the greedy. The beautiful Circe turned common shipwrecked sailors into swine, but you Americans allow your human swine to turn an entire population into grasping ogres. Is there no one with the visceral fortitude to tell the whole truth so that people can be possessed of virtue?

ECCENTRIC. There is virtue here, Socrates. Civilization makes strides, though on balance you can view your own civilization superior to our own. Automobiles, aircraft and tall building lifts do not create a better life, or virtue. Most troublesome, we have lost the faith. We no longer think without first discerning the "correct" thought. That is a greater sin than thievery or debauchery. If we lie to ourselves, how can we do different than lie to others.

SOCRATES. Well said, old man. Still, during my visit here, I have learned that the make-believe world of communism has unraveled. And you still must seek a leader who is willing to look at GATT-based free international trade and ask, *What kind of fools are we?* Foreign capital from Japan and

Arab nations—where hatred of America has achieved an art form—is now buying up your institutional arrangements, and stands ready to make economic decisions for your country, all because of a child-like faith in theory period instruction. I must learn more about this Roosevelt. Why did not distress produce the earlier remedy, namely tariffs and the return from distress described by your Andrew Jackson, your William McKinley, and so on? Why did your Calvin Coolidge become imbued with the free international trade spirit and guide his nation toward ruin? What is this doggerel I find pasted in one of your library manuscripts?

> A stranger stood at the gates of Hell,
> The devil himself answered the bell.
> He looked him over from head to toe,
> And said, "My friend, I would like to know
> "What have you done in the line of sin,
> "That entitles you to come within?"

Why this lack of respect for Roosevelt? Is there anyone who understands this man Roosevelt? Please direct me to someone who understands Franklin D. Roosevelt. I do not wish to speak to ministers and government functionaries. I hunger for different fare.

The last words on the scroll were, "Here, Socrates, take it." We assume the eccentric meant the tape, but some scholars believe a candy bar was offered to the man from ancient Greece. The scroll on which the foregoing dialogue was found had a margin note near the end. It said simply, "Two Roosevelts, one awarded the Nobel." Scholars believe this note had reference to America's greatest promoter of war, Theodore Roosevelt, who was given the Nobel Peace Prize. Socrates seems not to have discerned the sardonic humor of the Swedes, who later awarded Henry Kissinger the same

Nobel Peace Prize after he annihilated vast blocs of Asian population and their real estate. There was one other line, "Warren G. Harding," followed by the commentary—"Nothing."

5.

Sisyphus, the king of Corinth, edged his way into The Lost
Dialogues *with a mere mention of his name. One not familiar with
the story might wonder why Socrates would compare the Corin-
thian to Franklin D. Roosevelt. Yet there is a connection, no matter
how nebulous. For Franklin D. Roosevelt saw his country being
carried away, much like a beloved daughter. That, perhaps, is the
meaning of his "ill-housed, ill-clothed, ill-fed" line. Roosevelt went
to the river gods called big business and was told un-American
forces had kidnapped his country exactly the way Zeus carried of
Aegina, the agency for this mischief being protection for American
producers. Likely he was told that cousin Theodore Roosevelt's
quest for empire was waylaid by the same forces. Roosevelt com-
plained that this was not the entire story, thereby angering the
great Zeus of international piracy, for which reason F.D.R. was
sentenced, like Sisyphus to roll a great stone uphill. Each time it
reached the summit, it was kicked loose to roll down hill again. No
compromise, no logic could alter the rules under which the great
Roosevelt governed. More radical observers saw Roosevelt as little
more than a puppet, a great American destroyer who finally opted
for war to make secure his place in history. The last stanza of the
anti-Roosevelt poem Socrates asked about was recorded as a codicil
to Scroll #5. The poem itself was Socrates' first exposure to the
concept of Hell as opposed to Hades.*

> Now Franklin D. talked long and loud,
> And the devil stood with his head bowed,
> At last he [the devil] said, "Mr friend, Let me make it clear,
> You'll have to move on, you cannot stay here [Hell].

*Socrates also noted—in the margin—that some numismatists
unfairly refer to the Roosevelt dime as "The American Destroyer
issue."*

The Curse of Sisyphus 49

This dialogus is not typical of Socrates. For once, he allows another to govern the discourse. He presents himself as more student than teacher, and yet his icy logic intercepts and evaluates everything. As a marginal note, the intelligence was forwarded via Scroll #5 that C.I.A. operatives used sophisticated sound apparatus to record this dialogue. A Freedom of Information Act request for a transcript was made by the publishers, and denied on the basis that no such document existed. Yet the Scroll transcript was mailed to Socrates anonymously within two days after this meeting. He took it with him when he returned to Athens.

THE CURSE OF SISYPHUS

SOCRATES. I learn through my interrogations that this man, Franklin D. Roosevelt, inherited the consequences of an unusually clever political maneuver to enshrine free international trade. Who knows the virtue of this man?

EX-OFFICIAL. I do, Socrates. I served in his administration as a bureaucrat, and I can tell you that he had but one qualification for high office: he wanted very badly to be President and do good for his people. I do not know whether he understood the difference between being stumbled over or kicked. He inherited a government—to use his words—under which he could see "a third of a nation ill-housed, ill-clothed and ill-fed." I leave it to you to discover whether this was a result of free international trade cemented into place by the Wilson administration, and the conversion of the Republican Party to the ideals and policies of the slave-holding South.

SOCRATES. The arguments I have encountered so far tend to pique my interest and engage my analysis. Did this President Roosevelt reject the slaver's free trade as logic would suggest, or was he forced to labor like Sisyphus under shadow powers?

EX-OFFICIAL. He engaged advisers and they infected him with rhetoric exactly opposite the reasoning of the great Presidents and Senators of the past, from Washington to Webster, from Lincoln to William McKinley. Franklin D. and his associates invented a new nomenclature for free international trade—Reciprocal Trade Agreements. Using this approach, he and his Secretary of State, Cordell Hull, were able to sidestep the Constitutional requirement that trade treaties be ratified by the Senate. In any case, Senators were no longer named by state legislatures by this time, and therefore they took little or no direction from the political forums of their constituency. Rather than closing the gates of economic mischief, Roosevelt kept them wide open. As a consequence, the Great Depression did not end quickly.

SOCRATES. I am sure I should have asked this of the oeconomist, or even the archivist or street critics I have met. Surely the record can establish whether this import invasion was significant?

EX-OFFICIAL. Between 1933 and 1943, our excess ot imports of farm products over exports amounted to about ten entire crops of wheat. That is, all the imports of farm goods, translated into terms of wheat, show that the so-called surpluses were imported. Wheat is the key to thinking in composite terms because it is the chief crop for which public policy maintains production in excess of domestic disappearance. If sugar and red meat are imported, and if feed grain acres are displaced, and if wheat acres are therefore pressed into service, then the so-called surplus syndrome is really a matter of dislocation, or imbalance, not surplus.

The Curse of Sisyphus 51

Suppose that the imports had been all corn or hogs or cotton. During a decade when hogs were being liquidated on bonfires becaue of over-production, the U.S. imported 5.5 billion bushels of corn. In terms of hogs alone, the importation would have been 250 million head weighing 200 pounds each. In terms of cotton, the imports during that decade would have amounted to 66 million bales weighing 500 pounds each. In other words, if all these imports had consisted of a combination of corn and wheat and hogs and cotton, the import situation would have read two crops of corn, seven crops of wheat, one and three-fourths crops of hogs and four crops of cotton. If the American farmer had been allowed to produce the amount of agricultural products that we imported, it would have, conservatively, required fifteen million able-bodied men the entire eleven years to have produced these crops and hogs. The high prices of American industrial products made the cost of producing cotton so high in this country that when the growing of cotton was successfully developed in other countries the American farmer lost his world markets for raw cotton. The introduction into the United States of cheap agricultural products from fertile countries with cheap labor was bound to lose the American farmer his home market not only for cotton, but for his wheat, his corn, his meat, and every other farm crop and product. And that is exactly what happened.

SOCRATES. I cannot believe that the infrastructure I see and the apparent prosperity of the people is a consequence of the debauchery you describe. Was nothing done to restore prosperity to the countryside?

EX-OFFICIAL. Once, during the long decade of the 1930s, the government took a knee-jerk saving action. Corn, the farm commodity staple usually compared to an hour of labor for parity purposes, had declined in price to ten cents a bushel. It was raised by edict over four times higher. The improvement in the economic countryside was fantastic. This experience made secure the proposition that income was simply a product of production times price. Obviously, no production times whatever the price means no income. Full production times a full price means an overall income sufficient to consume the production. Therefore a debilitated price times full production is no different than drought or hail in annihilating income.

SOCRATES. Are you suggesting that natural calamity does not enhance prices?

EX-OFFICIAL. In a business equation with availability and sales interrelated—your supply and demand—there is a cause-effect relationship. But this is seldom true for the entire economic realm. Socrates, free trade conditions govern: if low cost areas of the world are allowed to rupture prices for the United States, as during a non-tariff era, then surplus inventories develop. The low prices that are imported with these inventories create a shortfall of income, and the lack of buying power then creates surpluses.

SOCRATES. This all seems terribly confusing. Let me go back to this man Roosevelt, a Democrat, and a follower of the slaver's free trade policies. Was there not a great conflict? Did not this same man lead agriculture and industry out of the chasm, for so I have been told as Zeus is my witness.

EX-OFFICIAL. Free trade worldwide created a depression worldwide, and there were resultant wars, the inevitable byproduct of free international trade. Allow me, dear Socrates, to sketch for you developments since your own time. You will discern, of course, that the changes are in scope only, not principle, and not unlike the trade wars between Athens and Cyprus, or the Levant and Egypt in your own time. These businesses you call pirates have challenged the state itself since time immemorial. Between Sparta and Syracuse, between England and the industrial world, the pirates—excuse me, I find myself using your grammar—rather the cartels have sketched boundaries and assigned spheres of influence, often with the assistance of state departments, somtimes in defiance of them. As for lesser states, these are traded like dime bags of popcorn or other business assets. I can assure you, dear Socrates, that modern wars all have had an economic origin. There may have been a time when men fought for food and survival. Nowadays they struggle for markets, and this points up the fundamental defect in any unbalanced system: deficiency of purchasing power.

SOCRATES. You, then, suggest that a failure to distribute the purchasing power needed to absorb the production of industry, mining and agriculture at full employment in fact accounts for too many goods—you say, overproduction—and the export market provides relief: often at the cost of war. And that is what your oeconomist calls access to foreign markets, a right you seem to claim because the foreigner is extended similar rights to dispose of goods in your market, often at ruinous prices. It would seem to this Athenian that non-industrial people have even less purchasing power than your people, thus the so-called balance of trade is an illusion. Does this not explain why great exporting powers literally refuse to collect, even if possible, thus gifting their production?

EX-OFFICIAL. Exporters do not gift, Socrates!

SOCRATES. Ah, but they do, not at their own expense, but at the expense of those who purchase foreign bonds, which in due course become worthless.

EX-OFFICIAL. Yes, I see!

SOCRATES. So you will confirm for the record of this conversation that the struggle for markets is manufacturered by a chronic deficiency in purchasing power?

EX-OFFICIAL. The United States became involved in a war with both Germany and Japan, a war that was sought and choreographed even before I left the administration. When it happened in response to American provocation and Japanese response, there was a general feeling in the Congress that without structural balance in the economy, the United States might go broke in the middle of the war and lose the war.

SOCRATES. What does this mean, "go broke?"

EX-OFFICIAL. It means to lose the ability to function, to pay for material used to fight—arms and food, for instance. It means the exchange equation breaks down.

SOCRATES. How was this danger dealt with?

EX-OFFICIAL. Congress passed a Stabilization Measure. This meant basic storable commodities from 80% of the harvested acres were restored in price to the pre-1929 level. Many semi-storable commodities were treated the same way. And, of course, other raw materials were driven back to parity by speculators who hoped to enrich themselves by the war.

SOCRATES. But without tariffs to protect your producers, did not ship traffic from the four corners of the earth bring ruin, as has always been the case?

EX-OFFICIAL. No, Socrates. The enemy surrounded the United States and kept most imports away. They had ships that sailed under the water, and in fact did the U.S. a favor by intercepting and sinking foreign ship traffic. With farm commodities at par with wages for workers and the cost of capital in balance according to indexed figures, prosperity returned, even while a war was being fought. We have an income tax in the United States, now a very high tax. Had we had an average tax of 15% during World War II, the revenue gathered in would have paid for the war by the time of its termination.

SOCRATES. Then you must have rediscovered the fallacy of unfettered free international trade. Have you not lapsed again into the same old pattern—your people greedy for cheap products from the neo-slave producers of the world?

EX-OFFICIAL. Yes, Socrates, we lapsed—or perhaps it would be more correct to say we merely had a recess in the program to ruin America. You see, the Wilson-Roosevelt maneuvers were not set aside. Quite the contrary, the champions of free international trade prevailed even while their successes seemed blunted by a world conflict. Shortly after World War II, the Congress struck down parity, making it necessary to increase public and private debt year after year.

SOCRATES. I see. This business of borrowing money into circulation, then withholding more money creation to make payment and debt service impossible! I understand it because it was the same scheme that haunted Persia, then cursed Greece and Rome.

EX-OFFICIAL. Yes, and later on it annihilated the defense of Carthage, and can be said to have presided over death and wars from the days of Deuteronomy to the eve of the 1948 Presidential election.

SOCRATES. This 1948 election, was it a significant turning point in your political demise?

EX-OFFICIAL. Yes. The Congress voted to have done with the business of supporting agricultural income. By that time Harry S. Truman—the politico who assumed power upon the death of President Roosevelt—had invited into the government so many Council on Foreign Relations members, they literally installed their neo-slave ideas on free international trade for all time. The precursor for GATT (General Agreement on Tariffs and Trade) came into being in 1948. And free trade entry into the United States for both raw materials and finished goods was allowed, causing a resultant falloff in employment and rural survival.

SOCRATES. Were there no voices in opposition or for modification of this drastic turn of events?

EX-OFFICIAL. Certainly. Congressman Al Gore Sr., fought for a bill to preserve full parity for another year for basic storable commodities. Earlier, out of the Senate came the Aiken measure to press agriculture back to the world level from which it had been rescued by WW II. And also there was the Brannan Plan to socialize agriculture. This meant allowing commodities to flow into trade channels at world prices, and giving growers, selectively, relief checks to pace the rate of farm bankruptcy.

SOCRATES. But other than alms, nothing was done to check the free international trade being promoted by the nabobs of privilege?

EX-OFFICIAL. Free trade has not been challenged seriously, except by the underworld of economics. Full parity for agricultural products was struck down by Ezra Taft Benson during the Eisenhower administration, circa 1952. This represented full retreat to the slaver's position held by Robert J. Walker. The old notion of a balanced period survived, buttressed as it was by more public and private debt each season! The Republican Party—except for minor issues—ceased to exist. And with that, we were off and running to oblivion. You can catch a thousand hints at the pace and direction of convulsion. But in my opinion a few statistics tell the story.

SOCRATES. What do the numbers say?

EX-OFFICIAL. The numbers speak with damning finality. The public and private debt stood at $555 billion in 1953. By 1960, it had doubled with to near $1 trillion. A decade later, the public and private debt figure stood at near $2 trillion, and by 1980 it was approximately $4 trillion. As we speak it has doubled and redoubled again, dragging in its wake the inevitable result. I submit to you a recent year. Income from all raw materials was $318.8 billion. It should have been $664.17 billion, according to the parity formula. This meant that $608.72 billion new public and private debt had to be injected into the economy during this early year of the 1990s to keep the exchange economy from faltering. This debt obeys the laws of arithmetic and doubles and redoubles itself, much like a rabbit population, until there is not the wherewithal to feed the system—which will happen near the year A.D. 2000. Socrates, we have emptied the countryside in homage to free international trade. We have delivered ourselves like sheep into the hands of insensitive police, and we obey judges who are the enemies of reasoned law and freedom. We have come full circle. Having delivered ourselves into the free international trade mode, we no longer honor Washington. Instead we have turned unemployables into masters, and surrendered ourselves to their arrogant keep.

SOCRATES. Even in the face of this record, your leaders continued to reject the advise of your Founding Fathers.

EX-OFFICIAL. With gusto, dear Socrates. The NAFTA document, for instance, required 1,700 pages—741 pages for annexes, 619 pages for footnotes—all of which suggested special interests arranging matters for their own benefit. Between 1972 and the present, the U.S. lowered its tariffs from close to 40% down to 5%. This means, O Socrates, that we have had a silent depression for twenty years. During this period, deindustrialization has answered the steady drift toward free ineternational trade. And this trade has presided over a drop of inflation-adjusted wages for over 80% of the American population. In spite of the record the architects of free international trade continued their specious arguments—thus the GATT Geneva Round, the Dillon Round, the Kennedy Round, the Uruguay Round, and all the cockamamie schemes that attended the sellout of America. The setup sounded good as long as Mexico remained protected.

SOCRATES. Then this land called Mexico, too, has lost its will for self determination? Has no one pointed to the fallacy of opening its borders?

EX-OFFICIAL. There are always people who argue for a saving action. They have identified the fantastic disruption

that would attend opening of the borders—soaring unemployment, an economy faltering much like East Germany because of the sudden withdrawal of support from
their own industries and intense competition from abroad.
Some critics of NAFTA even projected the great Mexican
migration that became inevitable as unemployment swept
Mexico. But it has to be remembered that the 20% of the
people styled as rich were bound to benefit from free international trade and synthetically lowered inflation. Unfortunately, inflation lowered this way is always preceeded by
wages and living standards lowered even more.

SOCRATES. Logic makes me tend to agree with what I have
heard so far. Yet still, a lack of virtue cannot be the only fault.
I know a casino and a government produce nothing. Somewhere, somehow, there has to be a harvest from Mother
Earth. But how can people removed from a tryst with nature
fully understand this harvest money, which surely must
spring from barter, or transactions many times removed
from the original transaction? Finally, have we ignorance
here, or thoroughly informed self interest? Like Diagones of
old, I require more light, honesty—and virtue.

*A margin note added the fact that Socrates was being followed
when he parted company with the ex-official.*

6.

By the time Socrates assembled a record of his sixth dialogue, made a matter of record on Scroll #6, he was being watched by American Jannassaries—agency men in the employ of the F.B.I., the C.I.A., even the ubiquitous A.T.F. The last, on one occasion, must have searched Socrates for a joint of marijuana, a most difficult task considering that his garment had no pockets. Socrates entered City College of New York, easily passing through the electronic surveillance device, and started reading Plato's The Trial and Death of Socrates, *a compilation that included the* Apology, The Discourse of Crito *and select passages known to the literary world as* Phaedro, and Euthyphro. *He got halfway through the* Introduction to Euthyphro *when a young school-man approached. The young man introduced himself sotto voce and agreed to order up a phonetic transcriber to "hard copy" the gist of the conversation. He ignored an F.B.I. agent standing in a nearby stack of books. There were a few preliminary notes, all cryptically recorded in parenthesis on Scroll #6. Then the opening line.*

SOMETHING FOR NOTHING.

SCHOOLMAN. Ignore him, Socrates, for he knows not what he does. If he hears, he will not be able to comprehend the meaning of our conversation. Unless we anger the powers that be, he is harmless—even useful, for he is at least employed and feeding his family, and not on relief. As for myself, I am tenured.

SOCRATES. Yes. I understand that tenure is sacred in American academia.

SCHOOLMAN. I will smile on that, my friend. The ability to

smile denotes a certain power, and now I extend this power to you. I hear the answers you have received during your visit have not been satisfactory.

SOCRATES. Not entirely. I know that I am to be tried and executed upon my return to Athens, and even the wealth of Midas, the King of Phrygia, could not save me. I will be accused of being giddy with knowledge, virtue if you will, but this alarms me not. I will be accused of being anti-democracy, and I will have to plead guilty. The untrained mind will ratify almost anything as long as the discourse is soothing, like a fine brew. Moreover, crafty liars infect the truth in a democracy and handle it as something relative and malleable. For instance, I have sought to understand banking, and I find the supply of lies to be infinite. My dear teacher, I am perplexed by the paradox of money and banking. I will surely speak to the Assembly when I return. What can I say?

SCHOOLMAN. The truth, Socrates. No less.

SOCRATES. It must be admitted that the private minting system called banking relies on a full measure of public gullibility? Yet you take pardonable pride in your scientific system. Your alchemists have unveiled secrets vastly more recondite than the mystery of money. How is it, then, that you will not ask the simple and obvious question you command of every pupil in a basic course of study—"Where does it come from, and where does it go?"

SCHOOLMAN. Ah, this is a question that cannot be asked or answered within the rules of scholarship.

SOCRATES. Is this intimidation not a relic of barbarism? And has it not so numbed the population that few, if any, believe private mints create dollars and destroy them at will for the purpose of secret pocket picking and speculation with the public's money without their knowledge? The industrialists and farmers who are called upon to answer this money creation with production seem to be dupes.

SCHOOLMAN. The money creation professionals take the position that their secret minting of money is a vote for the future. They see their venturesome acts as a public service that enables men and enterprise to be financed, also existing business to be financed, and agriculture to have seed money for the next crop.

SOCRATES. Yes, but is this not done at the expense of and without the knowledge of the community. So this defense is not only self-serving, but absurd. It has all the earmarks of an unauthorized private tax on the citizens of the realm. Further, it sets up an immediate benefit, then finally the ultimate ruin of the favored few.

SCHOOLMAN. Where do you perceive a fallacy, O Socrates?

SOCRATES. It is obvious that the men so financed, the enterprises so expanded, the farmers so assisted, in fact pay interest for their loans as though they were real loans instead of new journal entry money created at the expense of the rest of the community. I beg to tell you, the science of mathematics has not been annulled because you have the instruments I see everywhere—your FAX machines, computers, copy instruments, even the tape recorders that often take down my words, or the phonetic transcribers that are creating a manuscript of these dialogues for my benefit. I will agree that our system of gold and silver has its difficulties, but nothing like the malaise I see.

SCHOOLMAN. Then you reject the analyses so far revealed?

SOCRATES. Not entirely. But I must say, I have heard little reflection on the inversion that has overtaken individual capitalism. Even your own John R. Commons, who cries *institutional arrangements* at every turn, seems never to have probed the physical requirements analysis, and stops short of saying, I *seek virtue* first. But I analyze an arithmetical problem in terms of mathematics, not motives, intentions or rascality. The problem is much more serious than watching the second hand of the conjurer as he performs with the first.

SCHOOLMAN. Meaning?

SOCRATES. Nature presides. Her grip of mankind is secure. We cannot control the science of life with legislation, even though simpletons try to legislate biology. By under-standing it, you seem to seek a flaw in the price system, and well you might. But first I must lay bare the flaw in the money system. Having been instructed by your contem-poraries, I now see that a slip in the bookkeeper's craft has governed the brew of Hades your civilization has become. This slip is so elementary a child can explain it for what it is—a mistake as basic as an arithmetical blunder.

SCHOOLMAN. My dear Socrates, I must ask you to digress enough to explain what you see?

SOCRATES. For the sake of meaningful dialogue, let me separate the awesome problems of stimulating production and abolishing poverty, unemployment and homelessness from the money matter. Our Greek society has proved the possibility of stabilizing stagnation. Your own United States proved it in the 1930s. So let me tell you my answer. Wealth immobilized in a productive system must be paid through abstinence from consumption. Owners of money may contribute a part. But most capitalization must be met by a surrender of the right to consume. These conditions observed, the revenue of wealth can be expanded ad infinitum. It is because the genuine initial abstinence is burked that the existing system is what it is.

SCHOOLMAN. Are you suggesting that loans be abolished and capital formation relegated to hard savings?

SOCRATES. Listen well, dear teacher! Entrepreneurs can place on deposit collateral security and vow to pay usury. In turn they can have money created for their purpose, all this being done at the expense of the community. I cannot fathom this, or postulate the existence of even one Athenian who would accept such an abuse of reason. Nevertheless your people bear this burden without complaint, even handing over their miserable savings for the purpose of participating in usury's return. This willingness to endure does not confer on the system the logic it requires to endure. For as I perceive the scheme, this creation of productive power does not create the money required for distribution. This flaw is doubly troublesome when production is assured the foreigner, and free trade transports goods to people who earn less than necessary to consume. A failure by industry to distribute money condemns full distribution of the product by the laws of mathematics.

SCHOOLMAN. Yes, without parity the distribution of income breaks down, not only for farmers, but for labor as well.

SOCRATES. As organized via your money system, capital is communal debt, not wealth. You cannot solve the conundrum by free trade or by tariffs without first rejecting the illusion that great benefits are bestowed on the community by the monetary system, which at face value is as dishonest as uttering false coins or tampering with weights and measures. This monetary fiction—this business of tampering with money, creating it, destroying it, merely permits some people to get something for nothing at the expense of the many.

SCHOOLMAN. Even so, broad-spectrum distribution of land meant broad-spectrum distribution of income as long as a fair share of the population still had forty acres of virgin territory.

SOCRATES. Yes. And this observation finds common sense rapport with the free trade syndrome. When the act of production fails to create the credits needed to consume the production, free trade is invoked as an expedient to support employment at home. The vision of transferring unemployment to the foreigner, of course, is the predominant cause of war. To correct the abomination of war—which now has achieved cosmic violence—it becomes necessary to correct the shortfall in consumer buying power. And correction of this deficiency in paying power cannot be corrected without correcting the creation of money scheme. I marvel that grown people possessed of thought and reason stand up in broad daylight and cannot see that the remedy for want and war are the same.

SCHOOLMAN. Do you mean to suggest that production depends more on gestation and seed-time and harvest and several industrial equivalents, and not on bankers pretending to lend money?

SOCRATES. That much is gainsaid. Capitalization—by the republic or by the individual—must be matched by abstinence of consumption to equal the value of capitalization, or the same will be accounted for dishonestly by banking's sleight of hand, and this latter lowers the value of money. This has the effect of treating wealth in the pipeline as consumption wealth because the banker has the power to drain it out to repay himself, thereby creating the dislocation th⌃t cries for free trade and ends in war.

SCHOOLMAN. Socrates, you have taken several seven league strides since you first posed the question, *What is a dollar?* Oh, I have heard of your meeting with one of our economists. *The Wall Street Journal* would not report it, but the newsletters and the underground press—(look at the F.B.I. man, he is craning his neck to the breaking point trying to pick up our words. . . lower yours, my dear Socrates, we will have our sport with this abuser of the Constitution).

SOCRATES. Yes, I whisper, so be it! Now I must impale on the syllogism of logic a fact even a child not yet the age of reason can see. When money is first issued, that first exchange of created money for wealth makes it possible for the utterer to get something for nothing.

SCHOOLMAN. Not true if the money is backed?

SOCRATES. No. Not true is something valuable, gold for instance, is incorporated in the money token.

SCHOOLMAN. Perhaps this is why President Wilson, having made the mistake of supporting the Federal Reserve, said the following in 1916. "A great industrial nation is controlled by its system of credit—our system of credit is concentrated. The growth of the nation and all our activities are in the hands of a few men. . .who can chill and check and destroy our economic freedom."

SOCRATES. Now you understand the genius of a Republic, for your democracy is destined to die, strangled by a few obscure people operating in the shadows. You hear the recondite pundits speak of monetary policy, which expression should annihilate their position. Not even an incarcerated lunatic would speak of a weights and measure policy. There is even a greater fallacy afloat, and it can be undone only by comprehending the observable fact that *capital is wealth already consumed,* and that therefore dead debt must be unburdened, this to encourage new wealth for fresh capital. Free trade has too little to do with production and distribution, and too much with speculative profits. After all, the policeman who issues summons—much like government—produces nothing.

SCHOOLMAN. You agree, then, that economics at all levels must obey physical laws?

SOCRATES. I agree. Certainly not metaphysical laws, or laws beyond the physical. This can be examined, but it must not take on the tone of apology. It seems superbly ridiculous to speak in hushed tones about the absurd as though it were real. On the other hand, the torturers of reason compel citizens to forgo individual thought without appeal to a higher approved authority, and on the other hand individuals without virtue seek to gain perpetual revenue without a further expenditure of energy. There is no simple remedy. The world may choose austerity rather than plenty. I confess some confusion. Money, not monopoly, is the prime problem?

SCHOOLMAN. Socrates, know that Adam Smith argued for free international trade because the Lords owned everything, and the general population lived lives of near total degradation. We hear the argument that free international trade will pull the monopolies off their high horse. There is just enough truth here to make that proposition dangerous. Certainly there are better ways to insure rivalry among domestic companies—anti-trust laws, for instance. Unfortunately, the answers to all our changes are encased in browbeating and headcracking, and in cheap shots from academia and government officials and their industrial patrons. The last seem to benefit from monopolistic protection of one sort or another in any case. Withal, free ineternational trade—in view of any historical perspective—has to be the worst of all commercial policies, but it has as a close second the protection of monopolies, which has made a shambles of U.S. policy. In the U.S. no effort has been made to break up the giants. The Sherman and Clayton Acts—which were designed to do just that—might as well not exist.

SOCRATES. Whatever the course of human events, the role of virtue is to understand. I must now discover why mature people permit this awesome transaction whereby creators of money get something for nothing with the community being ignorant of the consequences.

SCHOOLMAN. It was not always so.

SOCRATES. No. In my own Greece, gold is money, which you will admit complies with the rules of physical reality. I will reflect on this.

A special note was appended to the transcript of Scroll #6. It said that a special alarm was sounded at C.C.N.Y. Library at 6:30 p.m., just as an unidentified schoolman ushered Socrates outside the view of a G-man on duty to protect the Athenian. Apparently

Socrates left the establishment through a door used by janitors, and eluded his protector agent. The alarm was silenced after an hour, and two hours later the emergency was called off.

7.

When Socrates was detained—not arrested—by the F.B.I., he had in his possession one of the transcripts now known as Scroll #6 of The Lost Dialogues. *The document was classified as* TOP SECRET *and never returned to the Athenian philosopher. He had neither money nor credentials on his person and was cited for illegal entry into the United States. Socrates was interrogated for hours without counsel. A young Greek scholar he had come to know posted bail and promised Socrates would appear in Magistrate's Court as scheduled. At that time, Socrates knew he was in residence on borrowed time. While constructing his own version of the F.B.I. interrogation, the second copy of the conversation—the one seized by the F.B.I.—was delivered via a Greek sympathizer. It is now classified as document Scroll #6.*

Scroll #7 was composed of material taken by Xerox from the pages of a book, then joined with questions and answers as best recalled, no recording or transcribing equipment being available. In this instance, Socrates met with a physicist who once upon a time worked on the Manhattan Project. He declined to furnish further intelligence to this project for the development of cosmic destruction even before the end of World War II, for which reason he has been shadowed by C.I.A. operatives ever since. He met Socrates at a hamburger stand when he heard the philosopher say, "Only in America is every meat sandwich done to death because of government edict." Thus the name Jack-in-the-Box made the transition to Athenian Scroll #7, fragments and parts of which are presented below.

WEALTH IS ENERGY

SOCRATES. It is true, is it not, that every hamburger must now be cooked to charcoal because of an eatery accident in one of your outback states?

PHYSICIST. Yes, my friend, it is true. The guardians of American health have presided over the health profile sinking from first in the world to twenty-sixth, and this entitles them to take stern measures. Therefore it is no longer possible to buy a medium-rare hamburger. No one seems to care about the origin of the hamburger, only about how it is distributed and served.

SOCRATES. A point in question. Where does it come from, this wealth and income that all societies seek to tax and redistribute and control, even to how meat is cooked? And where does it go if it is not living or immortal?

PHYSICIST. Without going beyond the physical and into the metaphysical—into ontology, theodicy and the like—there can be only one answer. Wealth is energy, and it can only come from the Sun, usually through the agency of photosynthesis in plant life. Sometimes this energy is stored in fossil fuel reserves for a few hundred million years, and recaptured by technology—our oil, gas, coal, and so on. In the main, the energy required to stoke the metabolic furnaces of human beings is harvested on farms. Human beings and farm animals consume this energy; and of course give it up via respiration.

SOCRATES. Then life is a struggle for energy?

PHYSICIST. Yes. Nowadays we believe in the evolutionary process. This process, in a word, must be considered parasitic. That is, higher life forms feed on lower life forms.

SOCRATES. Are you not feeding on more original sources of energy? Your coal, oil, natural gas?

PHYSICIST. Yes. Most work nowadays is done with machines fed by such fuel.

SOCRATES. This is most troublesome, for it seems that this new dimension to productivity could not favor food production and the production of raw materials of organic origin?

PHYSICIST. O Socrates, I must acquaint you with our laws of thermodynamics. These are not legislated laws, rather scientific laws. I have to refer to them because they embody great generalizations about energy, common denominators, if you will, that define how energy applies to machines as well as living beings, and communities. The laws of thermodynamics answer your question, *Where does it come from, and where does it go.*

SOCRATES. And what are these strange laws?

PHYSICIST. The first law rejects the idea that there can be perpetual motion—human or machine. Work cannot emanate out of a void without a supply of energy. A human being cannot live without food. An automobile cannot run without fuel. A factory cannot run without power.

SOCRATES. I have examined an oeconomist as to the meaning of a dollar unit of account, which seems strange to me. Is there an energy unit of account?

PHYSICIST. There certainly is, O Socrates. There is a scientific unit of heat energy known as the *calorie.* This is the heat energy required to raise one pound of water 1.023 degrees Fahrenheit, or one kilogram one degree Centigrade. These are measures for temperature. We also have a unit for power, *horsepower.*

SOCRATES. This seems odd, for surely horses are of different breeds and sizes, and would therefore accomplish different amounts of physical labor.

PHYSICIST. That is true. But in our scientific era we define horsepower as the power it would take to lift 550 pounds one foot in one second. The calculations can be quite complicated. Suffice it to say that it takes one million calories to feed a working person one year. This energy, of course, is harvested from agriculture and sometimes from the sea.

SOCRATES. I believe I understand your most intelligent point. Energy powers all agencies for doing work. Therefore the Sun is the capital forming agency—so that is where *it* comes from. But where does *it* go?

PHYSICIST. Ah, now the second thermodynamics law comes into play. In performing its task, whatever it is, energy is consumed or decayed. It cannot be used twice.

SOCRATES. Very well. Perpetual motion is impossible. And the wealth created by energy must also decay in the fullness of time. How then can money in the hands of a person confer perpetual revenue on the holder? It would seem to me that such consumable wealth is "consumed" even as the energy used to create this wealth is created. I perceive that there is really no connection between the money monopoly and the requisites of life. Therefore the real attraction of money wealth would seem to be the power it provides the creditor over the debtor.

PHYSICIST. You are most perceptive, O Socrates. An understanding of the *physical connection* does not rely on accepting the institutional arrangements for ownership or the flim-flam of the monetary system. It should be clear that the hunter-turned-farmer was and will always be the first laborer and capitalist, and as such—anatomically, and economically—he is the first to hire and pay himself. As late as 1800 in the United States, a farmer hired himself and only a fraction of another worker. By 1923, this same composite farmer hired himself and two other workers—and this pattern continued, governed by the state of the arts. Briefly stated, we have to say this "dealer with nature," this farmer and miner, hires all other labor in accordance with an immutable economic law requiring energy harvested from nature, and wages and prices suitable for exchange at full employment and production. To the degree that labor and agriculture are shortchanged, to that degree we invite poverty, insecurity and revolution. While others continue to synthesize economic activity with debt, and intervene as seems best to keep the worst effects from showing, the physicist is forced to invoke logic and realize that physics and the laws of energy govern. We think it is responsible behavior to recapture the logic and values of the above stated reality, starting with—"And the earth cooled."

SOCRATES. The attempts to defeat the laws of physics give rise to the clashes with logic you speak of?

PHYSICIST. Yes. The final act of our present international play started in 1948 with the passage of the Aiken Bill, and that series of events that struck down the mathematical requirements for a balanced exchange equation. You should read about how some lawmakers fought to keep full parity because they understood the anatomy of income creation and the role raw materials economics played in the maintenance of a solvent economy. You might then be able to see that the biggest and most effective reserve the U.S. has is rural America. Now with GATT, NAFTA, APPA, (American

Products Produced Abroad), the scuttle-parity scenario has become a theory period item, and a delusion pursued by all presidents since Truman. Socrates, the fall of Troy via the admission of a wooden horse was no more ludicrous than the Trojan Horse we've admitted into our government. According to our present delusion, agriculture no longer counts. Foreign trade does. Tourism does. Riverboat gambling does. The lottery does. The casino does. And the epitome of economic progress is perceived to be socialization of investment via money creation and higher taxes for the middle class.

SOCRATES. It would seem, then, we are obliqued to make a distinction, first, between productive enterprise that delivers wealth to the community, and, second, between an individual's wealth and the wealth of the community—in terms of physics, of course.

PHYSICIST. That is correct, Socrates. You see, in Daniel Boone's Kentucky community, all production was accomplished strictly for home consumption. In our society, production is for exchange. In this context, consumption is often seen as a shortfall, for the real driving force is to accumulate certificates of wealth.

SOCRATES. But under your certificate system, individual wealth seems to be no more than national debt. That is why—to use your word—boondogglers in universities and courthouses, who provide purely imaginary services, lay claim to participation in the national wealth. So do actors and sports figures, and ticket writing policemen—even the vicious Jannasaaries among your C.I.A. terrorists.

PHYSICIST. You follow my logic. I am a physicist. I do not deal in imaginary quantities. In government and in banking, the negative quantity seems to be a fixture. But from the physicist's point of view, the least number of cows or pigs is one. In mathematics they use minus figures so it is no accident that debts bow to mathematics, not physics.

SOCRATES. Indeed, debts seem to have a religious hold on labor, much like slavery, since they do not decay and are not consumed, as is energy in the process of living. On the contrary, they grow according to the strange rules of compound interest. And compound interest is as impossible as doubling and redoubling of hummingbirds or cattle or those strange bacterial workers I am told are operative in soils. So now I perceive that there is great confusion in the minds of most people between wealth and debt. Your society seems to be administered not for creators of wealth, but for manipulators who furnish want. So your traders create famines, and your great business houses create war. Thus, I have confirmed for myself, has assumed control over the lives of mortals.

PHYSICIST. As William Petty put it, Labor is the father and Earth is the mother of wealth. But how do you tell this to a fence post? There was such a fence post who wrote in 1909, one H. D. MacLeod. He saw debt as wealth creation, and therefore wealth was no more than a product of the mind.

SOCRATES. I would say this man was a goose. With his mental facilities that addled, no wonder he confused speculation with wealth.

PHYSICIST. Then you see the paradox, dear Socrates?

SOCRATES. Yes. Wealth can come only from the raw materials of the Earth because they are collectors of solar energy. Lenders, at the expense of the entire community, effect a change in production, albeit not in consumption credits. This sleight of hand in effect gives a piece of property two owners, and if this is accepted outside of a lunatic colony, then MacLeod is correct, indeed, and wealth can be created out of nothing much as your Federal Reserve pretends. Please tell me more.

PHYSICIST. I can only quote another great physicist, one Frederick Soddy, a Nobel Price discoverer of physical facts that finally gave us the atomic bomb. He wrote of MacLeod, But, heedless of the fact that, *even in his day, money was no longer necessarily specie or made of any precious metal, but might be, as now it mainly is, a mere paper acknowledgment of the community's indebtedness to the owner of the token, he fell into an error greater than that he ascribed to the Mercantile System in his own definition of wealth.* [At this point Socrates made several Xeroxed pages a matter of record, for they conveyed the long quote he hoped to take home and which he could not commit to memory with certainty.] "Money, being the instrument of an important public purpose, is rightly regarded as wealth, but everything else which serves any human purpose and which nature does not afford gratuitously is wealth also. . . Everything therefore forms a part of wealth which has a power of purchasing, for which anything useful or agreeable would be given in exchange," [quoting MacLeod]. [This is as complete a confusion between wealth and debt as was ever made by the ordinary untrained mind, and the error vitiates all economic reasoning to this day. Exultingly, H. D. MacLeod pounced upon it, and with the utmost hardihood pushed it to its logical conclusion. He twitted the earlier economists for hesitating to include a merchant's Credit (or ability to run into debt) as wealth merely for fear of being forced to admit that wealth can be created out of nothing. This did not worry him. He defines pure economics as the science which treats of exchanges and nothing but exchanges.] "A merchant's Credit is purchasing power exactly as money." [Therefore, according to Aristotle and Mill, Credit is Wealth. In the grip of this syllogism MacLeod warms to his subject, and proceeds to demonstrate that wealth *can* be created out of nothing. But before quoting from him a few words of introduction an explanation may be helpful. Let us now quote a few extracts from MacLeod's *Theory of Credit*:] "How is a Debt created? By the mere consent of two minds. By the mere *fiat* of the Human Will. When two persons have agreed to create a debt, whence does it come? Is it extracted from the materials of the globe? No. It is a valuable product created out of Absolute Nothing, and when it is extinguished it is a valuable product decreated into Nothing by the mere *fiat* of the Human Will. Hence we now see that there is a third source of Wealth besides the Earth and the Human Mind, namely the Human Will. Goods, Chattels, Commodities, Wealth can be created out of Absolute Nothing and Decreated again into the Absolute Nothing from whence they came, to the utter confusion of all the materialistic philosophers from Kapila to the present day and to the first school of Economists. The superlative importance of these considerations will appear when we come to exhibit the mechanism and practical effects of the great system of Banking." [And of this system . . . he was already able to say: "At the present time Credit is the most gigantic species of Property in this country, and the trade in Debts is beyond all comparison the most colossal branch of commerce. The subject of Credit is one of the most extensive and intricate branches of Mercantile Law. The merchants who trade in Debts—namely Bankers—are now the Rulers and Regulators of Commerce; they almost control the fortunes of States. As there are shops for dealing in bread, in furniture, in clothes and every other species of property, so there are shops—some of the most palatial structures of modern times—for the express purpose of dealing in Debts; and those shops are called BANKS. "And as there are corn markets and fish markets, and many other sorts of markets, so there is a market for buying and selling Foreign Debts, which is called the Royal Exchange. Thus Banks are nothing but Debt shops, and the Royal exchange is the great Debt Market of Europe."[The interest about all this is that MacLeod—an acknowledged authority on the theory of Banking and Credit—is merely more candid than the economists in his treatment of this question. He is quite correct in pushing the definition of wealth as adopted by John Stuart Mill and *other economists to its logical conclusion, and in proving that if wealth is what can be bought and sold it can be created out of nothing in defiance of the laws of physics*. It is the economist's definition of wealth that is at fault and which vitiates the conclusion. If we reasoned similarly in physics, we would probably discover that weights possessed the property of levitation.]

SOCRATES. I do not believe Plato would agree with this goose. I know him well as a student. He is not addled, and I challenge those who would use his name in vain to support the distortions they heap on civilization. Plato understood credit in a physical sense, and he would never violate reason.

PHYSICIST. Socrates, in the usual meaning of the term, credit implies relinquishing money to the borrower, giving up its power in the process. But the bank with its credit gives up nothing, though the community does, and the borrower receives it. It is for this reason that Federal Reserve chairmen have testified that "without debt there would be no currency." Isn't it ironic that the better educated classes prefer the abstraction called money to real property, but the banks insist on real property when they create and loan out money (should I say credit?) based on collateral.

SOCRATES. The elements of your statecraft are now falling into place for this tired old Greek. You tax your people beyond endurance and spend most of these revenues for what you call defense, or shouldering your international burden. Having ignored the laws of physics, you have become, as of September 16, 1985, a debtor nation, and the international money power—born in France before it shifted to London and New York—moved to Japan, making you the yellow man's burden.

PHYSICIST. Now you see history's cycle. The Roosevelt you should have been studying, namely Theodore, sought an American Empire, not so much to own every spit of land, but to construct a transfer system for taking money from the people via the Treasury and giving it to defense clients who in turn purchase the right kind of lawmakers and President. This business equation came into its own with World War I and World War II. When I became mature enough to understand the real purpose of war, I resigned from the Manhattan Project. I saw its racist overtones, and I understood slavery. Henry Adams alluded it to the role of the people in a democracy. He said "the only question" was whether the prolitariat was to be purchased and sold with bread and circuses, or handled with force. The legacy is easy to identify. We pretend to support democracies around the world, but in fact it is the dictator who draws largess from the American Treasury as long as he keeps his people in thraldom. The cycles of life and death govern in the long run, but we have always man's witless intervention to contend with. So far civilization has not produced leaders with the intelligence to govern in tune with the requirements of the cosmos, and for this reason the crafty bend affairs to their own end, and not to benefit the many. This contains the seeds of its own destruction—thus convulsions at regular intervals in history.

SOCRATES. So much for your country's indignant charge that the Greek society relied on slavery. I see a more pernicious slavery housed within your debt system than any in ancient history, and I see it enlarged to include the rest of the world. And now I have cause to wonder how secure are your much recited personal freedoms. I bow to your freedom of speech, such as it is, but I am distressed that so many people do not have the wit to use it. I will have my scribe, your citizen, my friend, make a recap of this conversation. Should I succeed in communicating what I have learned here, I will have achieved virtue beyond compare. I realize I am out of warp, and this implies that what I have learned will be frozen in time and released as the science of physics requires.

Socrates was detained again by the C.I.A. upon parting company with the old Manhattan Project physicist.

8.

The cell was damp and dark. A turnkey kept to his cubicle and didn't trouble himself to look in on the prisoner scheduled for hostile interrogation in the morning. There was only one other prisoner in this strange C.I.A. "safe house," and Socrates made contact soon enough while the terminally bored turnkey played his ghetto buster at decibles high enough to penetrate concrete and rebar.

A FINAL CLASH OF WILLS

PRISONER, A MUSICIAN. Your fame precedes you, O Socrates. They want the secret of how you defeated time, and they will get it or kill you trying. Be careful about what you say. This place is bugged, and what is said is surely recorded.

SOCRATES. I am now seventy years of age. What I say is for all to hear. I know not whether death is to be preferred to the ear-shattering obscenity vibrating through these walls. Is death a state of nothingness, or the point at which the soul migrates from one world to another? If you suppose the former, a state of sleep not even disturbed by dreams, how can it be other than a blessing, for eternity is but a single night. If death delivers one from state agents such as incarcerated us here, then virtuous Judges such as Minos and Rhadamanthus and Aeacus and Triptolemus await the traveler, for what pleasure? I would meet death a thousand times for a word with Homer or Palamedes or Ajax or any other man who has suffered unjustly. I cannot say, *Only in America do they put people to death for asking questions,* for it is a worldwide malaise. But surely this cacophony I hear is the worst of all. What is it?

MUSICIAN. I am a musician, and I see and hear in these sounds the onset of degeneration, hastening as it were a final clash of wills. You will have detected faltering mental capacity amont the people, O Socrates. There are many reasons. Physicians see poor nutrition as a cause, and surely they are right. An old Kentucky agronomist once told me, "People can be fed to live peaceably or fight, to think or dream, to work or sleep, to be virile or pathologic, physically, mentally and spiritually developed or retarded, and any possible degree of advance or variation within the mechanical limits of the organism." Sociologists wonder about the absence of struggle in the lives of people. I see the debauchery of music as the last brick in too heavy a load for most human beings to carry.

SOCRATES. But I have heard beautiful music in your sound libraries, although I admit it seems unavailable among the populi. I even detect a warm charm backgrounding your old cinema offerings.

MUSICIAN. Yes, it was in the darkened classroom of the theatre that I learned love was a violin, trouble in the streets was modern jazz, war was brass and cymbals, worry and fear were cellos, bravery a trumpet call—and God, the Hollywood Bowl Symphony. Now newer forms have swept the field—rock, acid rock, heavy metal, rap, post modern, punk, new wave and so on. Do I offend you by calling such fare music?

SOCRATES. I am not offended. But I am intrigued by your veiled suggestion that deviations from musical norms are an anodyne for the "intense" feeling I see almost everywhere. Musician, tell me, is there a natural harmony, for I swear it must be so. I love the sounds of the gods, our music, and I sense that you once had such joys for the multitudes.

MUSICIAN. Oh, my, did we—for we had the great John Phillip Sousa, and the classics of Europe, the operas *Aida, La Bohéme,* the matchless music of Beethoven, Mozart, Bach. Now we have to endure sound effects machines, synthesizers, artificial pianos and trumpets. Generally, we do not think your state of the arts has discerned cycles and time—a fatuous assumption, I dare say. Does a mixture of too many cycles per second qualify as mucis in terms of nature's balance?

SOCRATES. I hope I understand, and with your help I hope to comprehend still more the role of debased music in this demise of civilization I see all around me. No, I do not think discordant sounds qualify as music.

MUSICIAN. Up to quite recently the natural tuning in classical music was 432 cycles per second on A and 256 on middle C—sound cycles, dear Socrates. This means the speed at which a vibration, say, from a lyre returns to its starting point in terms of times per second. Today, almost all music in churches is tuned at 440 cycles per second, for which reason the question is posed—*Does this have an effect on the human receiving instrument?* Beethoven, Mozart, Bach, all the classical greats tuned at 432 on A and 256 on middle C. This represents a natural shift for the human voice in singing—if music is properly tuned as a baseline.

SOCRATES. Yes, Plato understood these vibrations. The song of the bird harmonizes with nature, and I understand your tuning was so harmonized during a more civilized hour.

MUSICIAN. It did. The Belle Canto Choir—children who

sang in Italy—required young men to sing all their natural tuning voices at 432 and 256. The musical profession stayed with this tuning until after the American Revolutionary War, when the Council of Vienna took place. At that meeting, the oligarchies raised the tuning on a piano to 440 and even higher. The purpose for raising the tuning of musical instruments was to limit the thinking capacity of people.

SOCRATES. Surely your leaders understand that music is what ignites the divine spark to do creative thinking. It uplifts and confers a sense of well being. In the temple, beautiful music is at home because temple music is in tune with natural law—yes, we can agree on that. Why did the Masters of Music raise the tuning? Why did they perceive it necessary to bend the minds of people?

MUSICIAN. I believe you will find my answer contained in the discourse I now present. At the Council of Vienna the Masters of Music separated art and music from the sciences. Leonardo da Vinci said that art, music, science and geometry were as one, a trinity. But the Council's voice prevailed. This remained the norm until 1880, when Guiseppi Verdi—we call him Joe Green for fun—was elected to the Congress in Italy. He understood the importance of proper tuning and brought back into law 432 cycles per second on A. Tuning stayed at that level until the Treaty of Versailles in 1918, when an effort was made to change it—albeit with little success. Adolph Hitler and Joseph Goebbels raised tuning back to 440 for the purpose of mind control. The Beatles of England sang at 440 or higher, and the pop star Michael Jackson ran the tuning up to 445 and 450. There is now a movement of opera singers and classical musicians— including the first violinist for the Mozart Quartet in Europe—to bring back tuning to 432. Mozart and Bach played at 432. A violin tuned at 440 makes one feel the discomfort of the debased tuning immediately.

SOCRATES. Mind control! As if a lack of mental discipline didn't close down many minds!

MUSICIAN. It must be remembered, Goebbels and Adolph Hitler needed to mind-control people, and so they used the Romanist approach. Romanist music is not classical music. Romanist music is pitched higher. Music pitched at 440 or higher has a tendency to limit the ability to think because the music overwhelms. When a musical instrument is tuned properly, the human voice should be the primary thing you hear. When tuning is raised, this overwhelms the human voice, particularly when the music is loud. For these several reasons, rock and roll music has been called into question. The new musical forms are being pushed to destroy the principles that this nation was founded on. It is a movement to go to human secularism putting man above God. I might make the point that country-western music is not much better. Country-western music is despondent music, and this is what state slavers like. Country-western music says *Momma is in jail, Daddy is drunk and the baby has been run over by the pickup truck.* What is uplifting about that? Music is supposed to inspire people. It is supposed to trigger the divine spark, as you say. Beautiful music inspires people to do creative thinking. This is why classical music is so important. Jonathan Tinnebaum has scientifically proved that the spin of the earth, the hours, the minutes per second, all determine that 256 cycles per second on middle C is in harmony with God and nature.

SOCRATES. What has happened to music that was in tune with God and the world and with the political ideas of your

Founding Father Thomas Jefferson?

MUSICIAN. In our time church music has abandoned the classics. For instance, Wolfgang Amadeus Mozart's *Requiem High Mass* is no longer played. It is almost impossible to find a recording of it. In place of inspiring music, most churches have adopted cheap, tawdry ballads. If you want to limit a society in its ability to think, and if you want the society in a laissez faire mode, if you want people with a don't care attitude or an attitude that some people are just paupers or some people are going to be hungry and there are going to be diseases and famine and there is nothing you can do about it, when you reach this level of thinking in a society, you then justify those conditions to exist in your own mind. This is what has happened with the newer music, the free international trade, low cost producer idea that condemns most of the world to poverty status.

SOCRATES. Were the Beatles "accidental?"

MUSICIAN. Some observers say Beatlemania was planned and premeditated by the cult movement in England. It was reasoned that if tuning was raised to 440, 445 and 450, Beatle music could blow the minds of young people. LSD started in California and was all part of that same operation as the Beatles, this observation has it. Does this mean that music is being used to limit and destroy the republican form of government in America? Perhaps it is a defensible generalization to say that when one can do nothing, then the invisible hand of the market sets the price on cotton, on corn, or the invisible hand of the market is the reason why some people are hungry and poor, and why 60,000 plus people starve to death somewhere int he world each day. If that is the case, what is the use of planning and talking about doing anything about it? Under such conditions representation is no longer germain. And the citizen is merely a pawn in Kantian hands, ready and willing to surrender life when it is demanded from God the state.

SOCRATES. I feel a philosophical truth emerging.

MUSICIAN. When Leonardo daVinci in 1500 found the golden mean—based on the works of Nicholas of Cusa in the book called the *Doctrine of Learned Ignorance*—this intelligence was laid out based on the Christian and the neo-Platonic works of your student, Plato. He found that the minimum and the maximum is all one, like the Trinity. When Cusa and Toscanini went to work on this, they found the golden mean—from the top of one's head to his neck, to the middle of his stomach to the bottom of his foot, geometrically is the golden mean. This is the morphological growth of all living things. Everything that grows grows in relationship to the golden mean, plants included. This also defines the musical notes, *DO, RE, MI, FA, SO, LA, TI, DO*, that Plato understood in your time. This is also what Johannes Kepler found when he took Plato's five Platonic solids and put them inside a sphere and lined them up. He found the same relationship to the golden mean in the Sun, Earth, Mars, Uranus, Neptune and so on. They even found the asteroid zone which is the F sharp. It is no longer there.

SOCRATES. With men stripped of their mental maxima by strange levels of energy, the rejection of reason falls into place?

MUSICIAN. Perhaps. I do know that beautiful music when properly tuned at 432 on A and 256 on middle C—which complies with the scientifically natural law of tuning—inspires people and uplifts them. It confers creativeness on the hunan mind. A bill was introduced in the Italian legislature to bring tuning forks and tuning back to 432. They did bring it down to 440. That, of course, wouldn't mean a thing in the United States as far as most folks are concerned. Yet a number of opera troups in America are now playing at 432 and 256. Some of the church TV shows are beginning to identify this problem. The sway of music has gone far beyond God being the Hollywood Bowl Symphony. The book *Dope Incorporated* has laid this out in spades, including the cast of characters involved. It seems the operation with Ollie North was a drug operation. Ollie North and Richard Secord were bringing arms in from East Germany, flying them on U.S. planes into Central America and bringing dope back. As the opium merchants found out, any time you can lower the culture of a nation, you control a nation. If you can limit the ability of the average citizen to be involved in solving problems, then that is how you contorl them. During the American Revolution four Americans out of a thousand were all that could not read or write or do simple arithmetic. Today, probably 47% or more cannot read, write or do arithmetic. Forgive me Socrates, these are minor characters of our time. I cannot expect you to cluter your mind with their names.

SOCRATES. I have not criticized music. But I have chastised my countrymen for its overpowering tryst with sports. Thus the games and olympic contests where naked men and their trainers parade before the multitudes to take the minds of people off reality.

MUSICIAN. In Rome the government faced off men and had them kill each other. Here we have a different spectacle. In ancient Rome, some few people saw what they looked at. A few see what Cicero saw: "A bureaucrat is like a vulture.

Vultures are needed and bureaucrats are needed, but they are useless, shiftless, thieves, crooks as vicious as a little boy with a vicious dog. Who needs such creatures." We seem to have elected officials who have missed the whole point on how to think and how a republic is supposed to function. More important, it has been done by constructing a single political party system.

SOCRATES. A single party system?

MUSICIAN. Yes. It has two wings, and total agreement on major issues. Only on small, insignificant issues are there any disagreements. The population has become so anesthetized, few discern this reality. Therefore they vote one party in, one out—but the general debauchery of the Constitution goes on. The real masters of government have no great difficulty in maintaining control. Those talking heads in Congress, almost all are bought and paid for by the process itself. To gain election involves taking contributions, most of them from the industrialists and traders. Whenever a critical vote is taken, all these markers are called in. Once enough votes have been lined up to please—to use your term—the pirate-military-industrial-university complex, then a few are allowed to vote so as to please their constituents. At times some give up their sinecure to make good their bought and paid for agreement. All this has been accomplished by first wrecking the music, in my humble opinion.

SOCRATES. And in wrecking music, your intellectual advisers seek to wreck God. Now, with your discourse to reflect upon, I see why illiteracy grows by the hour, and is so appalling. Your religion—I mean your science—mocks man's first grasp for an understanding of his being, his soul.

Your hunt for control of nature has delivered cosmic violence, and your high priests believe they can have perpetual energy. Your science ministers learned *how*, but not whether you *should*. Without understanding the simple vibrations of nature these scientists have profaned the harmony of the universe. If only I could hear the divine sounds that brought civilization thus far. But I hear only the grinding of metal on a sore tooth—and they call this music. Small wonder that narcotics corrupt your young. The Father of Medicine, the great Hippocrates, said, "Let food be your medicine." But your healers rely on medicines—drugs, if you will—that will make a healthy person ill. How then can they make a sick person well? With bad vibrations to torment the psyche, and drug stores to train human protoplasm in the art of debauchery, is it any wonder that the country is awash in illegal narcotics?

The rest of the scroll was lost to the elements. Socrates did not sleep.The prison was lit brightly, with the intensity of light gradually increased as the hours went by, for it was a trade practice to "condition" detainees for hostile interrogation.

9.

The interrogations started at 5:00 a.m. The chamber in which the questioning took place was refrigerated to an uncomfortable degree. It was windowless and entered only after Socrates had been kept standing for two hours in an equally cold hallway. Shackled hand and foot, the old philosopher could no nore than endure his pain stoically.

PERSUADE THE SEA NOT TO BREAK

AGENT NO. 1. So this is the great Socrates—or perhaps a whacko. We have them in New York and Washington—a dime a dozen. We wouldn't waste a glass of water on you, old man, except for the fact that you ask questions no one asks, and you come to conclusions that are a danger to the security of the United States. More important than that, we find no reference to you, no record of birth, no identification, no history—and yet you appear to be age seventy. This is not possible in the United States. Ok, let's have your name. Name?

SOCRATES. I am Socrates of Athens.

AGENT NO. 1. A Greek? How did you get into the country? Where are your papers?

SOCRATES. Sir, I gave my statement. I plead that you read it. I beg your understanding, for I do not know your customs. I will be gone in a day, with or without permission. [Socrates later wrote this note: My response infuriated my interrogators. Around me hostile faces and voices screamed as though I was surrounded by sharks in the Aegean Sea. A fist crashed into my forehead. A kick sent me sprawling. And then a man entered the room who seemed to have authority. He merely snapped his fingers and told all the others to leave. He helped me to a chair and offered me a drink, which I accepted.]

AGENT NO. 2. So you believe you will leave, *even though* you are bound "to a high-piercing, headlong rock in adamantine chains that none can break." Do you remember the lines? You should, Socrates—you see, I do not discard you as a looney off the streets. I see you as Prometheus, ready to steal fire from the gods to give it to common men. We can speak frankly, you and I, because

> Forever shall the intolerable present grind you down.
> And he who will release you is not born.
> Such fruit you reap for your man-loving ways.
> A god yourself, you did not dread God's anger,
> But gave to mortals honor not their due,
> And therefore you must guard this joyless rock—
> No rest, no sleep, no moment's respite.
> Groans shall you're speech be, lamentation
> Your only words.

Do you hear Zeus speak for today as for yesteryear?

SOCRATES. I hear. I can only say the words of Prometheus to Hermes, the Speedy Comer—

> Go and persuade the sea not to break.
> You will persuade me no more easily.

AGENT NO. 2. But what can it profit you, this knowledge you've assembled. Now you know how men of wisdom regulate politics. They provide death and war to catalyze production. O Socrates, we could stagnate much like ancient Greece. We could allow the raw materials of the Earth to dictate the level of prosperity. We could balance the exchange equation, but where would that leave the money creators and the service people who live well by this creation. No doubt these traitors you have been talking to have told you about the military-industrial-university complex. And that high minded physicist who wants to tear down the edifice that debt has built? What has he done for mankind, except to renounce the atomic bomb. Who has heard of him since then?

SOCRATES. Then it is true that since your Wilson administration, the forces of business piracy have invoked convoluted logic in order to dispossess the farmers and to command the economy?

AGENT NO. 2. Of course. This agency came into being because it was no longer a simple matter to create a spontaneous war. It took provocation and masterful politics to insert the U.S. into World War II, the populace was that peace-loving. Yet within twenty-four hours the American people changed form being the most peace loving to the most warlike on Earth. The potential has been fantastic ever since. Quite frankly, Socrates, we came to realize that we had to have wars. Lives have always been cheap. The raw materials of the Earth, they are dear. So what does it matter how many lives we spend to work the plan? You see Socrates, I really have no need to interrogate you. I know the answers, but I am not certain you know them—all of them. You have a secret, Socrates, and I need to know it. *Quid pro quo*, I am willing to share, but at the end of this interrogation I must have an answer. I know you well. You will not submit to torture or threat. And you have no fear of death. You proved that as a young soldier. I apologize for these Neanderthalers who abused you. They are used to dealing with peasants, and peasants understand only one thing—a club along side the head.

SOCRATES. I cannot accept your *quid pro quo*, not even if you offer pure knowledge.

AGENT NO. 2. I marvel at your tenacity, Socrates. You have mastered a most difficult subject, political economy. You have learned our language in record time. You understand why the second World War was choreographed even as the first was ending, and how Lenin was used to set up the war after World War I. But something happened, Socrates. The alchemists, as you call them, discovered the secret of the universe, and a naive President Truman ordered the A-bomb dropped on the crowded cities of Hiroshima and Nagasaki. This was a blow to us because we had succeeded in convincing people that America fought only for pure and high ideals. Now, America, the white hat in world affairs, accepted what we've always deplored, indiscriminate warfare on civilian populations, women and children included. Surprisingly, the people accepted this just as they had made the transition from peace to war within one day. Yes, people control with mind-bending music and drugs has been practiced with these tools. Clever, Socrates, you told us nothing via the prisoner—yes he was a prisoner—we inserted next to your cell. Know this, Socrates, we did expect to invade Japan. When that atom bomb was dropped, war material for half a million men was shipped immediately from Naha Harbor in Okinawa, half to Korea, the second half to Indochina, both for the next wars. Syngman Rhee and Ho Chi Minh became household words. You see, dear old Socrates, the powers of this world, the people I and the C.I.A. serve, cannot afford world destruction by atomic violence, but they have to have cozy little wars or there will be too small a market for products of an overindustrialized world.

SOCRATES. I have discerned as much, albeit I considered war an inevitable consequence of your economic rules, not your prime intention. I did not realize the killing art was being pursued directly as a game plan.

AGENT NO. 2. That is because you have not read the national Security Act of 1947. Lawyer Clark Clifford saw to it that the law would make possible a C.I.A. capable of creating and managing wars in tandem. Korea came on schedule the day after John Foster Dulles concluded his meetings in Seoul. So you see, the Cold War and satellite wars became the equivalent of the big war as far as industrial manufacturers were concerned. With Korea on the drawing board even before surrender papers were signed aboard the battleship *Missouri*, the next act—annihilation of the family farm and the personal independence it represented—had to be accomplished. We could squeeze the freeholders between low prices and synthesized national income based on debt expansion.

SOCRATES. What about your Constitution? Did it not forbid Presidents to make war without the approval of your Congress?

AGENT NO. 2. Forget the Constitution. If we enforced it, all of our Presidents since Franklin D. Roosevelt would have had to be impeached and removed from office for sending troops into action without Congressional approval. The Constitution requires Congress to regulate the value of money, and otherwise maintain a standard for weights and measures. Can you think of a greater absurdity? Oh, we run up the Constitution the way we run up the flag so that the stinkfeet can salute. Only hopeless romantics cite its virtues. Our great Woodrow Wilson once lamented, too late, here, read it. "The masters of the government of the United States are the combined capitalists and manufacturers of the United States. It is written over every intimate page of the record of Congress, it is written all through the history of conferences at the White House, that the suggestions of economic policy in this country have come from one source, not from many sources. The benevolent guardians, the kind-hearted trustees who have taken the troubles of government off our hands have become so conspicuous that almost anybody can write out a list of them. . . The big bankers, the big manufacturers, the big masters of commerce, the heads of railroad corporations. . . The government of the United States at present is a foster child of the special interests." So much for the Constitution.

SOCRATES. You take unpardonable pride in bringing on the ruin of your country. Why? More important, why has no one stopped you?

AGENT NO. 2. *Quid pro quo*! Tell me what we must know, and I will tell you even who the real masters of government are. Oh, I see you are not ready. Yes, there are those who stood in the way. President Eisenhower believed he and Nikita Khrushchev could negotiate the Cold War out of existence, which would have been a disaster beyond immediate comprehension. He even ordered the U-2 spy plane grounded so as not to disturb his Summit. We sent it up anyway, and we rigged it to fail in the middle of Russia, scuttling the Khrushchev-Eisenhower peace attempt. Eisenhower never forgave us—but he was ill, so he accepted the blame personally, instead of hanging C.I.A. and others to dry in the

wind. He closed out his term of office by warning against a
military-industrial complex, a sop to his conscience. The
great unwashed never understood what he meant.

SOCRATES. Yes, I see. It really is not enough to understand
the mechanism, I must also understand the mendacity of the
barbarians. I have seen politicians in whose persons virtue
could be preserved with bread and discus throwers. But you
rely on wars?

AGENT NO. 2. Oh, absolutely, or beautiful conflicts—small
invasions like Cuba, and Iran, Iraq, Panama and Grenada,
bigger ones like Korea and Vietnam.

SOCRATES. Why did you supply Ho Chi Minh, and then fight
him?

AGENT NO. 2. You must understand, C.I.A. management is
fluid. We armed Ho Chi Minh to bring the French situation
to a head. This happened at Dien Bien Phu. With the French
impediment out of the way, we could engineer a million
person exodus from the North to the South in Vietnam, to
an area well below Saigon. This totally disrupted the
economy. By press releases and propaganda we managed to
turn these million displaced persons below Saigon into Viet
Cong. With that the balance sheets of the important companies were made. Let me illustrate. Helicopters cost us a
third our casualties, but the war literally saved that industry.

SOCRATES. Falling raw materials income, debt, war! I have
been told your President Kennedy wanted to dice the C.I.A.
into little pieces and drop them into the ocean. Is this true?

AGENT NO. 2. It is. More important, he ordered the issue of

currency outside the purview of the Federal Reserve. He also wanted out of Vietnam. He believed he was powerful enough to go head to head with the invisible government. In short, he was a raving man out of control. The order went out—and before long a trained team of shooters took him out of the picture, leaving a patsy behind and also a Warren Commission report for people who can't think.

SOCRATES. Why do you tell me these things? Why do you insult and betray your own? I have promised you no *quid pro quo*, and I intend none. So far you merely tell me that your government has become proficient in four areas: killing, stealing, lying and making wooden headed decisions.

AGENT NO. 2. One other—the control of people. You see, Socrates, we have a Social Security program. Most people will accept the loss of any freedom, endure any humiliation, any depraved action of government, any use of their sons and daughters on foreign battle grounds, as long as the Social Security program is left in place. Also, we maintain a constant drumbeat of entertainment for the purpose of achieving a mind-numbing effect. We can explain away anything just as our scientists can prove anything! I will give you an example. On or about September 1, 1989, an airplane, 007, stopped in Alaska. A former president of the United States, Richard Nixon, was removed as a passenger; and the plane went on its way, to be shot down by the Russians with two hundred sixty nine passengers aboard. The Cold War was faltering at the time. It thus received a new lease on life. Within a few days, the largest defense budget ever passed in peace time was made law. Do you think this spontaneous action just happened? Do you think that even one Social Security recipient objected?

SOCRATES. You may not intend it, but you confirm my gravest suspicions. I stand accused of all sorts of things in the comedies of Aristophenes. I am anti-people. I desire an end to democracy. I want only philosophers and brilliant people in government. There is not one scintilla of truth in these charges. I want only representative government much as your Founding Fathers envisioned it, not a one-man, one-vote government in the literal sense of the word you seem to have embraced. I have seen Athens decline form great prominence, based on a Republic, to carping mediocrity as an assembly of democracy.

AGENT NO. 2. For once I agree with you. Yes, we do like universal suffrage, not as once was the case with unit representation, but with as many litter cases as possible carried into the polls. We want the illiterate to count for as much as the most educated. Do you know why, Socrates? During the period when our great Presidents Johnson and Nixon dethroned the barbaric metal, gold, we conducted a well-constructed survey of voter habits. We found that of all the people who vote in a Presidential election, hardly 18% have a defensible rationale for how they vote. That's what we like to see in a democracy. The more addled, the more ignorant, the more handicapped the better.

SOCRATES. Then my musician friend is right, the American nation needs a second political party, not a third party, for as Zeus is my witness, you indeed have only one political party, and regardless of which wing is in power, it does what the management wants. But would a second political party based on your Constitution, and on a sound money system and trade equity, be able to wrest power away from the unseen people who govern from the wings?

Persuade The Sea Not To Break 101

AGENT NO. 2. No way, José. Even if a second political party tried harder—I cite the advertisement for a chariot rental, Socrates—such revolutionaries would not have the expertise required for the people management we've perfected. Have you heard of Edward Bernays, the nephew of Sigmund Freud—no, of course not! He is one of our own. His 1928 book, *Propaganda*, said it all, and his ideas were crudely copied by the Nazi, Joseph Goebbels. Bernays invented, quote, his words, "the mechanism which controls the public mind and how it can be manipulated by a special pleader." He even convinced the liberals we should invade Nicaragua to save the interests of the United Fruit Company—how, dear Socrates? By keeping and adjusting a mailing list of no more than 10,000 American "opinion makers"—industrialists, journalists, professors, doctors, movie stars, the elite, my friend. "You've come a long way baby" was his slogan to hook women on tobacco. Fluoride for the drinking water was his—why? Andrew Mellon wanted it, otherwise, how do you get rid of a waste product that is more difficult to dispose of than atomic refuse? Bernays was a worthy predecessor for the company.

SOCRATES. Yes, your euphemism for C.I.A.

AGENT NO. 2. Yes, Socrates.

[Socrates added a note to the Scroll. "I listened to this braggadocio for hours that seemed like days. I heard about Malthusian population control for lesser nations, about war as the great stabilizer for civilization, about cunning men who sought to enslave, about McGeorge Bundy reversing the decision of his President during the Cuban invasion, and more. I fell asleep and was goaded into wakefulness. I cannot recall the detailed recitation of wars designed, won and lost by this sub rosa government. Finally I heard this man say. . ." At this point the recorder went on the fritz, for a time, developing a long unrecorded gap.]

AGENT NO. 2. Now, Socrates, I have given you the gift you have spent a lifetime pursuing, namely *virtue*, by which you mean *knowledge*. You now have "virtue" beyond all men, but you must settle your debt. So, you have no one with the status of a god to die for you and give you release. You have no Charon.

> Look for no ending to this agony
> Until a god will freely suffer for you,
> Will take on him your pain, and in your stead
> Descent to where the Sun is turned to darkness,
> The black depths of death.

SOCRATES. I know not what you want. If it is knowledge, I give it freely to all with the wit to listen.

AGENT NO. 2. No mortal man can live in our time and leave no trace as you have. We take you seriously, Socrates. We know everything, every invention, every art, every science, but we do not know how you managed to defeat time. You must tell me, *quid pro quo*.

SOCRATES. Should I possess this virtue and refuse to reveal all I know, what do you intend?

AGENT NO. 2. Let me give you a case report. After President Kennedy was assassinated, a Russian named Yuri I. Nasenko defected to the United States. We believed him to be a double agent. So we had him locked up in a safe house basement for *hostile interrogation*. This lasted for three years.

Persuade The Sea Not To Break 103

The poor man lost all his teeth in the process. Since Yuri was a witness in the Kennedy affair, it was necessary to confine him for the duration. This ended when the Warren Commission issued its report. Later we gave the Russian citizenship in the United States. We bought him a house and gave him a small pension. You see, Socrates, we can be generous, and you have no choice. Can you stand imprisonment at your age. Never mind the fact that you are willing, can your body stand torture? More important, can you stand your brand of virtue being erased for all time? Now, tell me, how did you defeat time and space?

SOCRATES. I will reflect on your question. But I must assure you, I will die in Athens. The book of this life has been written, and you cannot change it.

Apparently Socrates was remanded to a safe-keeping cell similar to the one that had accommodated Nasenko. When a guard went to the cell in the early morning, after the first full day of interrogation, Socrates was gone. The security system had not been touched. On the way out Socrates picked up the recordings of his night in the jail cell and the day-long interrogation. We must assume Socrates made his own transcripts, thus his inset notes. He had never done this before, always relying on students, thus we can suggest wide gaps in the dialogue, especially when the old man nodded off while the tape erased itself during the C.I.A. windbag's performance.

10.

Scroll # 9 of The Lost Dialogues *was the least damaged and the most complete. It was recorded by Plato with the understanding that the document become part of a Socrates time capsule, so to speak. It must be remembered that Socrates stood trial for corrupting the youth of Athens shortly after his unexplained absence. The bill of particulars that called for a trial has not survived antiquity. Nor has a transcript of the trial. We can be sure that Scroll # 9 figured in the indictment, for Socrates defended himself against Anytus Meletus and his associates, vile men who "took possession of your mind with their falsehoods," to quote Plato. Here Socrates spoke at an unnamed assembly.*

OF WIT AND VIRTUE

SOCRATES. Men of Athens, record well what I am about to tell you. I have returned from a journey to a far off land, one in which successful warriors are accorded the honor of a god. Indeed, they are made leaders of their nation at times, and the common people never tire of sacrificing their sons and daughters in foreign wars that seem a part of their national religion. In terms of the state of the arts, this nation is well advanced of our own. I will not trouble you with descriptions of wondrous chariots they have invented, or tell you very much about their towering buildings and crafts and sciences and their probes to the Moon. You would not understand, not being familiar with the grammar of the many subjects.

Men of Athens, we can learn from this race of slaves, for they are slaves, one and all. Each man and woman in the labor force works over a third of a year to support the commerce of war. Let me tell you how this penchant for war has been achieved. You will wonder aloud that grown men and women can be so lacking in mental capability as to endure the debauchery a few captains of industry have fastened upon them. The subtle way in which this state of affair was arrived at became my chief inquiry once it was apparent that I had been transported. They called their nation United States.

I am here to tell you that the Founding Fathers of that nation were men of wisdom, tolerance and fortitude. They discerned, soon enough, that specialists in the coins of many realms were challenging the civilization itself. A development most foreign to us had come to pass while those Founding Fathers were active. Great conspiracies of businesses called corporations—more powerful than pirate fleets or even armies—came to challenge the state. These trader corporations invaded the field of foreign relations, always considered the province of the assembly in our city-state. They assumed the status of international cartels. I know the word falls strangely on your ears. It is enough for me to relate that these cartels drew trade boundaries, allocated spheres of interest, and carved up the world among themselves, sometimes with legitimate governments and servants of certain states doing the bidding of these illegitimate masters. One such group of traders, supported by a nation called England, handled lesser states the way market hawkers sell vegetables to home economists.

The traders would undersell into the United States—rather the units that were to become the United states—using labor for craft creation that was kept in the most wretched of conditions. So the Founding Fathers, who were men of great intellectual achievement, declared themselves independent, and wrote a Constitution for the purpose of protecting the United States from import invasion.

Men of Athens, this nation achieved its destiny, and became the most powerful, the most advanced association of peoples on Earth. But alas and alack, men grew weary of paying out equitable sums for goods when foreign merchants stood salivating to sell at lesser prices. Thus, from time to time, this nation determined that its markets must be thrown open to the foreigner, and that government should do nothing in the face of foreign competition to protect its own, no matter what the dimension and shape of that competition, no matter what the consequences in terms of job losses, trade dislocations or crushed incomes. Each time such laws were written, misery followed. Each time free trade was repealed, prosperity became the common legacy.

Men of Athens, you will expect me to say that the United States came to the logical conclusion, and returned to its Constitution, but this was not the case. Cunning men invented a subterfuge that ran beyond instant comprehension. Money changers discovered they could loan out what they did not have because those who left their gold for safekeeping did not require its return all at the same time. In later years, these usurers uttered false currency to enterprising men at the expense of, and without knowledge of the entire community. That is how they broke down the buying power of the currency of the realm, forcing industry to hunt the world over for markets. And that, men of Athens, is how wars came to abandon ideology, and became oeconomic in origin. Yes, we have fought for food and loot, and to chastise a recalcitrant enemy. But these people of the United States have accepted war to accommodate monopoly organizations. I cannot detail the cleverness with which this goal was achieved. The U.S. Constitution was adopted in order to establish "for ourselves and our posterity" a par economy. Subsection 5 of Section 8 of the Constitution authorizes

Congress "to coin the money, regulate the value thereof, and of foreign coin, and to fix standards of weights and measures." Par economy is not possible without dealing with the value of money, not in terms of denominations printed thereon, but in terms of goods, commodities, labor that exchange for money. The third act of the First Congress was a tariff law to prevent cheap foreign goods and debased foreign currencies from determining the value of American money. It has always been the government's job to regulate that value. The value of money cannot be regulated without par exchange for the raw materials of the Earth. Here, in Greece, we rely on a niggardly supply of gold to stand in as a common denominator for raw materials.

The first characteristic of their industrial economy is division of labor. The moment farming became proficient enough to feed more people than the farmer had in his own family, there was a spinoff of labor now free to follow other pursuits. From that moment on agriculture became diminished in the number of persons involved in farm production, but agriculture still had the same economic function to perform.

All the early economists realized this. They have what they call Say's Law of Markets, that division of labor sets up reciprocal markets for each of the divisions of labor automatically. Those who farmed, for instance, provided the market for those who made tools—and those who neither farmed nor manufactured were in effect supported as a service industry by the productive elements in society. The justification for the school teacher, the guru, the policeman, the physician is seated in the fact that service industries allow farmers and manufacturers to be even more productive, having had service work taken off their hands. Oeconomists in effect said that since division of labor set up reciprocal markets, and since human wants could not be satisfied, there could be no such thing as under-consumption or over-production, or unemployment.

At the time of the United States Revolution against the nation called England, poverty was everywhere, just as it is now. Child labor flourished. It took two weeks of labor in a factory to earn the equivalent of a bushel of wheat. The nobles owned the land and they regulated farm prices above par of exchange. The man who made tools and wove cloth didn't earn enough to eat properly. Since labor couldn't even eat properly, there also wasn't enough money to buy industrial production—clothing, furniture, goods in general. This caused industry to embark on a policy that has ever been the curse of mankind—finding cheap raw materials for business production efficiency on the one hand, and selling to the high market of the world, wherever it was.

This is what the great tariff debates were all about in Henry Clay's day. I refer to an early American political leader. Finally, the decision was made to harness the American economy to Reciprocal Trade Agreements during the Roosevelt era—and this made it impossible to stabilize the American dollar in terms of American production costs and expenses for doing business.

Primary production—that is, taking raw materials form Mother Earth—came first. We can easily trace man from hunter to farmer. He took food and raw materials from nature, and the equation in terms of record keeping was *man debited, nature credited*, which represents a curious devise for maintaining accuracy. The farmer no longer made his own clothes or cooked his own spirits. He depended on the man in the city to handle this for him. That is what is meant by division of labor. But the only new thing that entered the economic equation continued to be raw materials, farm crops, iron ore, wool for a coat or cotton for a worker's clothes—man debited, nature credited! Division of labor aided efficiency, but in a physical sense manufacturing, trades, services simply added to the price, and not to the raw materials in the product. Except for farming, mining, fishing, etc., other equations in the economy read: man debited, man credited—a wash! There never has been and never will be a profit to an economy that does not read man debited, nature credited simply because nature is not paid back. I will lecture further on this at the lyceum next week.

Note that what I say is quite different from the oeconomics of an individual. An individual can make a profit at the expense of another, but the transaction is still a wash—forgive my American idiom—as far as the economy is concerned, man debited, man credited! If prices in exchange are at parity, production in fact sets up the credits for consumption of production.

Unfortunately, institutional arrangements—trading houses, banks, government itself—are used not to assure par exchange, but to enhance predatory business profits, or, in the case of government social programs, to keep the worst effects of predatory profits from showing. Thus they came to institutionalize poverty with low cost housing, relief checks, food stamps, and government as the employer of last resort. The game of pretend extended itself. The drones of society pretended that their work had meaning. The government pretended to obey its Constitution, and the people pretended they actually had protection under a Bill of Rights.

Men of Athens, unless primary barter power is set up as raw materials first enter trade channels, there is a failure. Unless this barter power is maintained at a foundation level, there is a failure. Only one concept answers this. That concept is the idea of a par economy, or parity.

You may wonder why institutional arrangements have intervened to prevent oeconomic parity between wages and capital costs on the one hand, and profits from business and agriculture on the other? Obviously, without relative parity, markets become promptly eroded, making it impossible for the oeconomy to consume its own production. The chief shortfall in this equation in the United States of America, agricultural parity.

This public policy has a sorrowful history. The idea that government can take away the benefits of a par economy with impunity has run the length of a two hundred year history in the United States. Only rarely have they seen flashes of brilliance. *If we buy the rails form England*, the great Abraham Lincoln told his advisers, *we will have the rails, but England will have our money. If we make the rails here, we will have both the rails and the money.*

Men of Athens, the international business and pirate houses have always believed that low raw material costs in one land and high markets in another constituted the royal road to greatest profits. These same houses always relied on a great spread between costs and sales domestically. Few realized that business principles are not the same as principles governing an oeconomy, and fewer still realize that principles governing an oeconomy ultimately govern with cheap labor from Europe and the Orient. In the United States, labor was successful in passing an immigration law, preventing entry to the foreigner much as we prevent entry to the Spartan. International business tried to circumvent the American cost level with cheap imports, and in the A.D. 1920s Congress passed a tariff bill so that cheap imports could not rupture the American price structure.

Thus stability for agriculture by its very nature was a constraint on what government could do. The greater the parity between different sectors of the oeconomy, the more difficult it is to enact laws, issue administrative decrees, rules and regulations, or make court decisions to revoke or abrogate individual rights, consequently the more restricted the domain of the bureaucrat and politician. A day came when the government employed more of the labor force than industry, and almost all defenses of freedom vanished.

Men of Athens, mark my words. Once free international trade became a benchmark of United States policy, the struggle of war was no longer for room, or for food, but for markets. The hunt for markets became necessary the day the United States gave away its own markets in order to be able to buy cheap foreign goods, then ended up hunting similar markets elsewhere. I discerned, during my visit, that under free international trade it is never possible to distribute enough purchasing power to absorb the product of any nation at full employment. Learned oeconomists call this situation "over production," though I suggest "under consumption" would be more appropriate. Thus the enchantment with export trade, usually called free trade, and the foreign market. These feints are highly competitive, and this keeps the drumbeat of war issuing its discordant sounds. Of course the lack of purchasing power is endemic. Non-industrial people have lower income potential, and therefore they cannot buy. Finally the most achieved oeconomy must tax its own in order to give money to the less developed so they can buy, a process that impoverishes the many and enriches the few.

Men of Athens, the cycles of war—and preparation of war—are merely a consequence of a strange money system, and the conceit that so few people can absorb economically the rest of a world filled with disparity. Only people in the underworld of economics—to use a term false teachers lavish on those who think for themselves—realize the truth of what I have revealed to you—that the wars of commerce have all been actuated by a struggle for markets, and by the obsession of an entire population with the accumulation of capital. I must say, free trade has not produced a virtuous mankind, rather a people that seeks perpetual revenue independent of a further expenditure of energy. For this hopeless vision they surrender their honor and their freedom. There are more police people—called cops—in the United States than there are full-time mainline farmers, growers who largely account for the food supply. The occupation of these cops, I discern, is to prey on citizens who venture onto streets and roads.

They have judges who have joined forces with ruinous taxation laws to fasten a form of judicial tyranny on the people. These judges are largely ignorant of logic and law, and provide great merriment to the people with their convoluted reasoning and the "Halloween" costumes they wear on the bench. They are always making political decisions, taking sides with the commerce of war to the detriment of common folk. Little scholarship or integrity attends the exercise of their office, for which reason legal anarchy has become the norm in lesser courts. They have tocsins and news media that prefer to make news rather than report it.

It has been calculated that Congress has 96,000 pounds of lawyers which are harder to move than a whale on dry land. [Laughter.] These "talking heads" would debate the propositions of Euclid rather than master the subject, and so they remain largely ignorant of their own history, and understand nothing of physical oeconomy.

Men of Athens, I have examined the evidence. I say it follows that oeconomics, calculated at the national level, is composed of two interlocking equations—payment by producers to their workers and themselves for producing new wealth, and then the payment of the same money by the same people and others to move the wealth out of the production system after it has been fabricated. All simple exchanges of finished property are only of individual importance. They add to the price, but not to the product.

Men of Athens, we can be assured that monopoly will one day seize the substance of the people. Human beings are what they are—if they have not virtue—and so the prosperous will seek to stretch out their prosperity by trading for their luxuries, and even their essentials, with races that treat their production slaves badly. This cannot but shortfall consumption at home. I cry for Athens when men think this way, as do our traders in the seaports and as do the learned men of Sparta. I reach out for that United States Constitution and the protection it afforded—as long as citizens had the wit and the virtue to keep it.

Men of Athens—we must seek virtue. We can do no less.

Socrates, the Athenian, was brought to trial in A.D. 399. There is no record of the trial. Indeed, Socrates did not emerge in the record until Plato and Aristotle published their journals. Scholars will never come to agreement over anything concerning Socrates. Accordingly, we are required to let The Lost Dialogues *speak for themselves. We can see that Socrates was more a republican than a democrat, republican meaning in favor of a Republic, democrat meaning in favor of democracy. He did not use the word "mobocracy," but he might as well have. He sought virtue, by which he meant knowledge, and he believed opinions have to be qualified. Whatever happened to him during his sojourn, Socrates knew he could not use virtue so acquired to undo the passage of events, even his own execution. Indeed,* The Lost Dialogues *could not plug in, so to speak, until after the events described therein had expired in the normal course of things.*

They have now expired. This means the insight of Socrates can now be used, if we have the wit and the virtue to use it! As for the secret of how Socrates defeated time and space, The Lost Dialogues *furnished no answer.*

INDEX

Failure to use the index device for novels has been one of the greatest deficits in American publishing, except in science fiction. Yet this should have been indicated for Report From Iron Mountain, *even for* War and Peace *and* Moby Dick. *Those who want to recall a favored page or passage in, say, James Michener's* The Covenant *can endure frustrations beyond comprehension finding the scene, the statement, the page, unless some Mickey Mouse marking or page bending device has been invoked. Thus this first. May others come to see that a book without an index should be denied a copyright.*

Warren Commission, 100, 104
wars, political, 95
Washington, George, 27, 28, 40
Wasps, The, 4
wealth, 72, 73, 74, 77
wealth immobilized, 64, 65
Wealth, already consumed, 68
Webster, Daniel, 16, 32, 33
Wells, H. G., xii
wheat, 8, 11
Wilson, Woodrow, 31, 34, 35,

40, 41, 42, 56, 67, 95
Woolley, C. Leonard, xi
World War I, 38, 96
World War II, 96;
    choreographed, 55

Xantippi, x
Xenophon, 3, 4

Zeus, 94
ziggurats, 10